Stories, Stats and Stuff About UNC Basketball

I0916336

Printed in the United States of America by
Mennonite Press, Inc.

ISBN 1-880652-81-1

PHOTO CREDITS All Photographs were supplied
by the North Carolina Collection, University
of North Carolina Library at Chapel Hill; the
UNC Sports Information Office; Simon
Griffiths; Ann Overton; and Jack Reimer.

TABLE OF CONTENTS

ACKNOWLEDGMENTS

When I agreed to write this book, I had no idea what I was getting into.

It quickly became apparent it would take more time and more energy than I ever imagined and I'd never get it done without the help of dozens of people.

Here are a few of them:

• The staff of Coman Publishing Company, in particular, to Stu Coman for giving me this opportunity, to Mark Panus for his guidance and editing, to Joey Mustian for his acute attention to details that I often overlooked and to Todd McGee and Jason Simon for doing my work while I was in Chapel Hill. And don't forget Greg Davis, Tommy Temple and Doreen Sanfelici for invaluable assistance with the technical work that I still don't understand.

• To Rick Brewer, Steve Kirschner and the UNC Sports Information staff, who gave me free run through their photo and media files. And special thanks to Matt Bowers and Kevin Best.

• To Dr. Jerry Cotten and his staff of the North Carolina Collection at the UNC Libraries.

• And last, but certainly not least, to Coach Dean Smith, his coaching staff and his office staff. Your support is truly appreciated.

It also became quickly apparent that it would be impossible to mention everyone who played a role in the success of the Carolina program.

One such person comes to mind immediately, and he deserves a mention on two counts. John Swofford has guided the UNC athletic program with a firm, but gentle hand for 16 years, yet has never received the credit he rightfully deserves. His friendship and support were instrumental in the writing of this book, and he gets no credit in it, either. Maybe, this will make up for it.

In researching the last few chapters of this book, one other realization struck home. That is that it is impossible to convey, in any sense, the impact that Dean Smith has had, on his players, on those around him, in the state of North Carolina and in the world.

What Smith has accomplished on the basketball court is mind-boggling. What he has accomplished off the court, away from the television lights and the glare of publicity, is even more impressive. He is a truly unique individual.

And last, there is my family. My wife, Rosemary —

without her forbearance, this book never would have been finished. She's glad it is, because now I have to clean up my office. My son, Charles — he's still waiting for me to get Jerry Stackhouse's autograph for him. And my daughter, Caroline — she can't wait for this to be published so she can show her UNC classmates the book her Dad wrote. I hope they all buy a copy.

In short, this book has been fun. I hope you have as much fun reading it as I had writing it.

— *Tom Harris*

ABOUT THE AUTHOR

Tom Harris has been covering Atlantic Coast Conference and University of North Carolina athletics for more than 25 years and has followed the Tar Heels even longer.

Born May 27, 1946, in Washington, N.C., Harris was hooked on the Heels in 1957, following Coach Frank McGuire's team through its 32-0, championship season. Harris graduated from UNC in the spring of 1968 with a bachelor's degree in psychology and, in July, became sports editor of his hometown newspaper, the *Washington (N.C.) Daily News*. He moved to Martinsville, Va., as sports editor of the *Martinsville Bulletin* in 1971.

In 1976, Harris left Martinsville to become high school sports editor of *The News & Observer* of Raleigh, N.C. Three years later, he moved to the college beat, where he spent 15 years covering primarily UNC and Duke. In his 18 ½ years with The *N&O*, Harris covered nine Final Fours — including both Tar Heel national championships in 1982 and 1993.

After leaving *The N&O* in 1995, Harris joined the editorial staff of Coman Publishing Company in Durham, N.C. in 1996. In August 1996, he was named editor of *HeelPrints*, a new Coman publication covering Tar Heels athletics.

Harris lives in Wake County, N.C., south of Raleigh, with wife Rosemary, a fourth-grade teacher, and son Charles, a freshman at Garner Senior High School. Daughter Caroline is a senior in the School of Journalism at UNC.

1910–52:
The Early Years

Intercollegiate basketball, like a late spring, was delayed in its arrival on the University of North Carolina campus.

Although Dr. James Naismith invented the game in 1891 for his classes at the YMCA Training School in Springfield, Mass., and within a few years the new sport had spread to campuses across the country, it didn't catch on in Chapel Hill until well past the turn of the century. Historians generally credit Wake Forest, Trinity (later to be renamed Duke, for its benefactor, tobacco magnate James B. Duke) and Guilford with fielding the first intercollegiate teams in North Carolina.

The first college game for which any written record exists was played Feb. 6, 1906, in Winston-Salem where Guilford defeated Wake Forest, 28-19.

For the first decade of its existence, basketball in North Carolina was played primarily at YMCAs, particularly in the cities of Winston-Salem, Greensboro and Charlotte. Charlotte was the state's hotbed, and it was there that the impetus for UNC's program was born.

The 1911 Tar Heels: (front row, left to right) Junius Smith, unidentified, Marvin "Philly" Ritch, John Hanes, Bill Tillett, (back row) Coach Nat Cartmell, Henry Long, Roy McKnight, William Wakeley and team manager Spurgeon Cook.

THE ATHLETIC "PROGRAM"

An ersatz football team had existed on the UNC campus since the early 1880s, and students had received permission to start a baseball team in the spring of 1891. A "Tennis Association," which led to a schedule of intercollegiate matches, also came into existence during this period.

In about 1895, school administrators, following the national trend, came to realize that a well-organized, wide-ranging program of athletics had its advantages.

J.W. Calder, North Carolina's athletic director at the time, introduced basketball on the campus in 1899-90, and by 1906, the game was being played regularly in gym classes. Dr. Robert B. Lawson, a physical education professor, provided the university with its first written set of rules for the game.

Of course, college administrators had no way of knowing the path the game would take or the importance it would assume, at UNC and elsewhere, within the next few decades. For them, basketball was a diversion, a healthy outlet for the rowdiness and hooliganism that affected college campuses.

THE CHARLOTTE CONNECTION

In 1910 a movement began on campus to field an intercollegiate basketball club. That impetus came from a group of students from Charlotte who had become familiar with the game through YMCA and burgeoning high school programs in the Queen City area.

Marvin "Philly" Ritch, a UNC junior, was the leader of the student movement, and he was joined in that effort by Cyrus Long, Roy McKnight, Junius Smith and Bill Tillett, all from Charlotte, and John Hanes of Winston-Salem.

"The boys from Charlotte just got together one day and started it," McKnight recalled later. "We practiced outdoors at first because the director of old Bynum Gym didn't want his pretty floor messed up. But we finally went to the administration about it, and he was ordered to let us use the gymnasium. We were outside practicing for a week until we got permission to use the gym."

Scheduling for the first season in 1910-11 was hit-and-miss, with games often arranged on a day's notice, or whenever a suitable opponent might be passing through the area. Opponents included "established" intercollegiate teams like Wake Forest, Davidson and Virginia, and YMCA teams.

Because of delays in arranging games, the team didn't play its first game until Jan. 27, 1911, winning 42-21 against Virginia Christian School.

THE FIRST COACH

Nat J. Cartmell certainly was not what anyone would envision as the "father" of UNC

Marvin "Philly" Ritch, who led the drive for an intercollegiate basketball team at UNC, disappears after the first season (1910-11). Although he's listed as a letter-winner that year, his name doesn't appear in any subsequent records.

TAR HEELS QUIZ

1. Name the six current ACC schools that were charter members of the Southern Conference in 1921.

Nat J. Cartmell, a world-renowned sprinter before becoming UNC's track coach in 1909, became the Tar Heels' first basketball coach in the 1910-11 season. He resigned in 1914, following his implication in a campus gambling scandal.

basketball, the progenitor of coaches like Bo Shepard, Ben Carnevale, Frank McGuire and Dean Smith.

Cartmell, in fact, was much better known in another sport. He was a world-renowned runner, a three-time Olympic medalist and one-time world record-holder in the 220-yard dash when he was hired as track coach by the University of North Carolina in 1909. He had won a pair of silver medals at the 1904 Olympic games in St. Louis while running the 100 and 200 meters, and followed up with a bronze in the 200 four years later.

He was a short, wiry, thick-chested man as were many sprinters of his day. He had an English brogue born of his upbringing in the Windemere region of England and a gift for the storytelling of his athletic exploits.

Cartmell came to the United States to attend college at the University of Pennsylvania, where he gained some fame as a football player and was exposed to the new game called basketball. He had returned to England in 1908 to compete in the London Olympics and to run in a series of European races, when he was contacted by Mike Murphy, who had coached Cartmell at Penn and had become one of his closest friends.

Murphy had heard that North Carolina was seeking a coach for its track team and wondered if Cartmell might be interested. He was. And for UNC, hiring a track coach with Cartmell's reputation was quite a coup.

Cartmell arrived in Chapel Hill in the fall of 1909, and about a year later UNC officials started to scour their small staff for someone to coach their fledgling basketball team. Of course, there was no money to hire a full-time coach; the athletic budget was less than $5,000 and almost all of that went to football, which also was the only source of athletic revenue. So, Cartmell got the job.

THE FIRST TEAM Surprisingly, the young Tar Heels fared well in their first season, winning their first five games and posting a 7-4 record.

Led by Roy McKnight and the Charlotte boys, the team followed its opening victory over Virginia Christian with wins over the Durham YMCA (60-18), Wake Forest (31-28), Davidson (27-25) and the Charlotte YMCA (42-28).

Each of those games was played in cozy Bynum Gym, which is today called Bynum Hall.

END OF AN ERA The 1912-13 team, which won four of 11 games, produced UNC's first "star" in Meb Long.

Led by Long, the Tar Heels improved to 10-8 with an expanded schedule in 1913-14. And for the first time, Carolina enjoyed some success away from Chapel Hill, winning games at Guilford and Elon and going 6-7 on the road.

Cartmell, however, barely lasted out the season. On March 21, apparently tipped off by an argument over a gambling debt, Orange County law officers raided a UNC dormitory room and arrested nine people — four freshmen, two law students, two townspeople and one faculty member (Cartmell) — engaged in a game of craps. A story in *The (Raleigh) News & Observer* two days later told of a floating gambling "ring" operating on campus that lured innocent students into games of chance and stripped them of their money.

University officials accused the newspaper of greatly exaggerating the situation, but all nine of the individuals involved paid a $25 bond and were ordered to appear in court in Hillsborough April 2 to face gambling charges.

On March 31, university officials announced the six students had been expelled and "Mr. Cartmell had severed his connection with the university."

On April 2, eight of the nine — one student failed to appear — pleaded guilty in court in Hillsborough and were fined. Cartmell and the two Chapel Hill residents — W.J. Patterson, a druggist, and Floyd Booker, listed as an "automobile man" — paid $20 plus court costs; the students paid $10 each.

Many in the university community, including all of the basketball players, considered Cartmell's transgression minor and the fine outrageous. The coach, though, left Chapel Hill in disgrace, eventually moving to New York state where he married and worked at various jobs until his death in the 1960s.

He never coached basketball again.

GROWING PAINS After Cartmell's resignation, Charles Doak, the school's baseball coach, was named basketball

The 1913-14 team was Nat Cartmell's last at Carolina. Players pictured are: (front row, left to right) Charles Tennant, unidentified, (middle row) Meb Long, Joseph Chambers, William Dowd, (back row) George Tandy, Coach Cartmell and Henry Long.

By "Raby" Tennant's own account, he and his brother Charles played together on the UNC team in 1914-15, making them the first brothers to play on the same team at Carolina.

coach. But Doak had neither the expertise nor the desire for the job, and in his second season (1915-16), the players took matters into their own hands. Led by Meb Long and George "Raby" Tennant, the team often worked out on its own, with good results.

The 12-6 record in 1915-16 was Carolina's best yet and included victories over Elon (51-14 and 19-15), Randolph Macon (47-18), Virginia Military (25-23), Davidson (31-21 and 20-14) and Guilford (40-26 and 51-21). The club closed with a seven-game winning streak, with five wins on the road.

THE HOME COURT

Bynum Gym wasn't the first basketball facility on UNC's campus, but it was the first used in intercollegiate competition.

No gymnasium existed on campus until 1885, although administrators had for years petitioned the state legislature and the Board of Trustees for a facility.

Finally, in '85, a gym was constructed near what is now Peabody Hall. It was a small building, with a 110-foot by 45-foot open area and, according to reviews, had "a splendid dancing floor."

Construction of a dedicated facility in which students could burn off excess energy was cause for great rejoicing among students and faculty. "Before this, four cases of insanity from overstudy developed, but there were none afterwards," one report said.

By 1896, however, the number of students again had outgrown the facilities, and administrators decided, against some opposition, to modify Memorial Hall for use as a gymnasium. Traditionalists considered such a plan a "desecration," but President Francis P. Venable argued that using the hall only once a year for graduation ceremonies was a waste of an otherwise useful building. The small gym, meanwhile, was renamed Commons Hall and converted into a dining facility.

Still, the need for a dedicated, multipurpose athletic facility increased as the student body continued to grow and athletic activity became more popular. Finally, in 1904 Judge William P. Bynum of Charlotte, a member of the state Supreme Court and a Davidson graduate, announced he would donate $25,000 for construction of a gym. The facility was to be named the William P. Bynum Jr. Gymnasium, in memory of Bynum's grandson, a former UNC student who died of typhoid at the end of his sophomore year.

At its dedication in 1905, Bynum Gym was one of the finest facilities on any college campus. It was "an imposing building of gray pressed brick with round brick columns. ... In addition to a spacious gymnasium floor, stocked with apparatus for exercise, the building contained a large swimming pool, locker rooms, shower baths and rooms for boxing and fencing, Swedish movements, anthropometric tests, and trophies."

Unfortunately, the "large

Long, then a junior, achieved what in those days passed for stardom. "Long scored more points than any other man in the Southern Intercollegiate Athletic Association," *The Carolina Magazine* reported.

BEATING VIRGINIA Doak resigned after the 1915-16 season, and for the first time, UNC had a coach whose primary athletic interest was basketball.

Howell Peacock was a star, on the basketball court and in the classroom, at the University of Georgia and came to Chapel Hill in 1915 to begin his training at the

Bynum Gymnasium, completed in 1905, served as the Tar Heels' home court from 1911 until 1924.

swimming pool" was not equipped with filters or circulating pumps. In 1914, it was declared unsanitary and unfit for use.

By 1920, the upper-level running track, which circled the gymnasium floor, was condemned, although it remained in use as a spectator area for basketball until 1923.

In 1928, Bynum Gym was renamed Bynum Hall and renovated for use as offices at a cost of $4,350. The building was renovated again for $46,550 in 1939 and served as home of the North Carolina Press and the UNC School of Journalism until the mid-1960s. Today, Bynum Hall houses the University Cashier's Office, the offices of the Dean of the Graduate School and the Department of Research Services.

UNC Medical School. He later became a noted surgeon.

He reluctantly accepted the offer to coach the Carolina team, but once he accepted, he attacked the job with scientific precision.

Peacock retained only two players — Tennant and Carlyle Shepard — from the 1915-16 team. His marketing tactics, though, brought in many new players, including Raby Tennant's brother, Buzz (Charles), who had played on the team earlier.

Peacock's efforts weren't immediately successful; his team finished with a 5-4 record in 1916-17. The team did, however, accomplish something that no previous team had managed — it beat Virginia.

The game was held on Feb. 24, 1917, in Lynchburg, Va.

The final score was 35-24. So monumental was the victory over Virginia that *The Daily Tar Heel* started a drive to reward the team, and eventually each of the 14 squad members was presented with a small gold basketball to commemorate the historic win.

THIN TIMES In the years leading up to and during World War I, all colleges suffered a shortage of athletic talent — players and coaches — and UNC was no exception.

Players and coaches often left for a year or two of military duty, then, if they were lucky, returned to pick up their academic and athletic careers, sometimes at the same school, sometimes elsewhere.

But, the military made contributions, too. In 1918, when Howell Peacock's medical studies forced him to

The 1920-21 team posted a 12-8 record and set the stage for a "Golden Era" of UNC basketball. Team members were: (front row, left to right) Monk McDonald, Howard Hanby, Billy Carmichael, Robert Griffith, Carlyle Shepard, (back row) team manager Joseph Person, Jesse Erwin, Ben Liipfert, John Morris and Maj. Fred Boye, coach.

give up coaching, the Tar Heels had a ready replacement in Capt. Fred Boye, a former West Point basketball captain who headed the ROTC program at Carolina. Boye remained for two seasons, guiding the Heels to a 12-8 record in his second year.

By the time Boye's assignment in Chapel Hill ended in 1921, however, the postwar boom was over, and no replacement was available. The team played without a head coach in 1921-22 and 1922-23.

THE SOUTHERN CONFERENCE

The 1920-21 season marked not only the beginning of a new decade, but also the beginning of a new era in Carolina basketball.

On Feb. 25-26, 1921, athletic officials from 15 Southern schools met in Atlanta at the urging of Al Doonan, head of the Atlanta Athletic Club. Doonan, and many others, were concerned that the Southern Intercollegiate Athletic Association was too big.

The SIAA had been founded in 1894, primarily to fight professionalism and establish eligibility rules for college baseball. UNC and current ACC members Clemson, Georgia Tech and Virginia all were charter members of the association, although Carolina and Virginia — regarded as two of the primary offenders in the use of ineligible (professional) baseball players — declined to participate.

An offshoot of the SIAA, the South Atlantic Intercollegiate Athletic Association, was formed in 1912, but its efforts centered mostly on track. A third group — the Athletic Conference of Southern State Universities, which included UNC and Virginia, was founded in 1915 and agreed essentially to leave eligibility questions up to the individual schools, which was the path UNC had followed all along.

World War I put eligibility questions — and therefore, conference affiliations — in the background until 1918-19, when there was a rapid expansion of athletic programs fed by a large number of physically active young war veterans. By 1920, the SIAA had grown to 33 schools.

Although football and basketball scheduling were the primary reasons for formation of the new conference, Doonan, one of the new league's staunchest proponents, offered to sweeten the pot. He promised to refurbish the old Atlanta Auditorium for a postseason basketball tournament to which all members of the new conference would be invited.

Fourteen schools — Alabama, Auburn, Clemson, Georgia, Georgia Tech, Kentucky, Maryland, Mississippi State, North Carolina, North Carolina State, Tennessee, Virginia, Virginia Tech and Washington & Lee — withdrew from the old league to form the new Southern Conference. Tulane attended the original meetings but delayed its entry until 1922, when Florida, Louisiana State, Mississippi, South Carolina and Vanderbilt also came on board.

1921-22: SOUTHERN CHAMPIONS

The Tar Heels were still without a full-time coach, but luckily they didn't need much coaching. In 1921-22, with Billy Carmichael and ball-handling wizard Monk McDonald joined by newcomers Curtis "Sis" Perry, Carl Mahler, Winton Greene and Billy's younger brother, Cartwright Carmichael, Carolina was loaded with talent.

And when the Southern Conference Tournament opened in Atlanta on Feb. 24, the Tar Heels were ready. They easily dispatched Howard and Newberry in the first two rounds, and then whipped powerful Georgia, 33-25. In the semifinals, mighty Alabama limited Cartwright Carmichael, UNC's rising young star, to a single field goal. Still, he hit 10 of 15 foul shots, and Carolina won 20-11 to advance to the final against Mercer.

In the championship, Cartwright Carmichael scored 18 points to lead Carolina to the title, 40-26. The Tar Heels finished the season with a 15-6 record.

THE FIRST ALL-AMERICAN While 1921-22 was a good season for Carolina, the 1922-23 campaign was even better.

With Cartwright Carmichael scoring at the phenomenal rate of almost 15 points a game (the team average was 36 per game), the Tar Heels ripped through the regular season to finish 14-0.

Carmichael was named to the Helms Foundation All-America team, becoming UNC's first All-American in any sport.

"He was the best basketball player I think we have had here," Monk McDonald recalled years later. "He was just as graceful as he could be. He could shoot from any part of the court. Cart looked better missing a shot than most players today when they make one. He had grace and skill and speed. He was just a complete ballplayer."

Tar Heel hopes for a second Southern Conference Tournament crown ended suddenly, however, in a 34-32 upset loss to Mississippi in the second round in Atlanta. The team finished 15-1, and dreams of a "perfect" season were delayed — for a year.

1923-24: HELMS CHAMPIONS

Norman Shepard, a 26-year old physical education instructor who had coached the UNC freshman team the previous two years, knew exactly what he was getting into when he agreed to become Carolina's varsity head coach in 1923.

"I had inherited a very good group of boys from the team before," Shepard said in Ken Rappoport's book

Cartwright Carmichael led Carolina to its first Southern Conference championship in 1922 and to its first national championship in 1924. He was UNC's first All-American in 1923 and also was a first-team All-American in '24.

Tar Heel: A History of North Carolina Basketball.
"Carmichael and McDonald were exceptionally good, and I had coached (Jack) Cobb and (Bill) Dodderer and (Billy) Devin on the freshman team. Carmichael and Cobb were so fast and quick with their faking and feinting and breaking, and Carmichael could drive for the basket with unbelievable speed and hold himself in the air for a long time, like he was suspended.

"Sportswriters in Atlanta were searching for adjectives for the beautiful defense our team played. They called us shadows and ghosts on defense."

The 1923-24 Tar Heels had it all. McDonald, at 5-foot-7, was the consummate ballhandler and passer. Carmichael was a slashing scorer and superb outside shooter. Cobb, a sophomore from Durham, was 6-foot-2, a giant in those days, with a deft shooting touch and unnatural agility for his size.

Dodderer, also a sophomore, was the "standing guard," the defensive specialist who seldom ventured past halfcourt. Devin, another sophomore, was pressed into duty when Winton Greene, a senior and the team's captain, suffered a leg injury early in the season. Jimmy Poole, a veteran from the '23 team, Henry Lineberger and Troy Johnston were the reserves.

Only Washington & Lee (which lost 19-16 on Feb. 8) and Duke (which lost 23-20 on Feb. 19) came close to challenging Carolina during the season. With Carmichael and Cobb leading the way, the Tar Heels entered the Southern Conference Tournament as the favorites.

The 1924 National Champions, designated by the Helms Foundation, included (front row, left to right) Jack Cobb, Bill Dodderer, Winton Greene, Cartwright Carmichael, Monk McDonald, (back row) team manager Gregory Smith, Jim Poole, Troy Johnston, Billy Devin and Henry Lineberger.

"Fast, accurate, shifty and clever," *News & Observer* editor Jonathan Daniels wrote of the duo, "both men are scoring demons as individuals but add to their powers as individual players the splendid co-operation that they have developed and they are invincible."

So it seemed. The Tar Heels easily handled Kentucky (41-20), Vanderbilt (37-20), Mississippi State (33-23) and Alabama (26-18) to win their second Southern Conference Tournament title in three years.

At the conclusion of the season, the Helms Foundation named both Carmichael and Cobb to its All-America team and declared the unbeaten Tar Heels (26-0) national champions.

ANOTHER TITLE Carmichael and McDonald graduated after the 1923-24 season, but McDonald stayed around to enter medical school and became the team's coach when Norman Shepard left to enter private business. Shepard is the only basketball coach in UNC history with a perfect career record — 26-0.

Cobb was back for his junior season, however, and better than ever. The '25 Carolina team wasn't quite as quick or quite as talented as the previous season's version, but it was good enough.

On Feb. 2, 1925, after winning nail-biters at Wake Forest (22-18), Duke (25-21) and Maryland (21-16), Carolina lost one — a 23-22 decision at Harvard. The loss ended a winning streak that had started at the beginning of the 1923-24 season, a stretch of 34 consecutive games.

The team's grueling schedule was solid preparation for the Southern Conference Tournament, though. After closing the regular season with five straight wins at home, Carolina swept past Virginia Tech, Louisiana State, Georgia Tech, Georgia and Tulane to win its second straight Southern Conference title.

Dour James Ashmore coached the Tar Heels for five seasons, posting an 80-37 record.

GOLDEN AGE REVISITED The end of the 1925-26 season, in essence, marked the end of a magical five years for Carolina basketball.

In the five seasons from 1921 through 1925, the Tar Heels won 96 games while losing 17. During that period, they went 19-1 in the Southern Conference Tournament.

Of the 17 losses, seven were by a margin of four points or fewer.

All of this was accomplished with a different coach — or no coach — each season.

"WHITE PHANTOMS" In the late 1920s and early '30s, Carolina often was called the "White Phantoms," and that moniker sometimes is associated with the 1924 team.

Actually, the term was coined after the Tar Heels' come-from-behind victory over Tulane in the 1925 Southern Conference championship game.

Atlanta sportswriter O.B. Keeler wrote of that game: "I wish I could find out the charm those five boys whispered, sitting close together on the floor, before they got up for the last charge. ... It must be good, for in that final whirling rush of the white phantoms, they shot six field goals in three minutes ... the most dazzling burst of scoring the entire tournament displayed. ..."

"White Phantoms" gained wide acceptance, and the

TEMPEST IN A TIN CAN

By the early 1920s, Bynum Gym had long since proved inadequate as the home of the North Carolina basketball team. The narrow playing surface — intended as an exercise floor, not a basketball court — was ill-suited for the faster game of the '20s. And the elevated running track, which served as the spectator gallery, had been condemned about 1919 but remained in use until 1922-23.

Finally, in 1923, the University's Building Committee approved construction of a new "Indoor Athletic Court." It was the first facility at UNC designed specifically for basketball.

The building was purchased from the Bland-Knox Company of Pittsburgh for $54,482.45, including construction.

The building was completed in the late fall of 1923, and students took one look at the shiny metal structure and gave it its name — the "Tin Can."

By today's standards, the "Tin Can" was spartan at best; but in 1923, it was among the finest campus facilities in the South.

It had locker rooms, showers, toilet facilities (small rooms built onto the sides of the building),

seating for about 1,500 spectators plus standing room, and it had a regulation-sized basketball floor, which most schools did not have.

What the Indoor Athletic Court did not have was heat. Pot-bellied stoves at each end of the building were woefully inadequate. The building was freezing cold in the winter and sweltering hot in the summer.

"In the winter, there would be icicles in the corners. You couldn't dress in there," a former Tar Heel player recalled. "It was so cold that we'd dress at Emerson Stadium about 300 yards away and run across Emerson Field (now the area between Lenoir Hall and Carmichael Auditorium) for games and practices."

Central heat was added in the mid-'30s, and the "Tin Can" was the site for all UNC indoor athletic events from 1923 until 1938, when Woollen Gymnasium was built. During and immediately after World War II, the "Tin Can" was used for barracks-type housing for soldiers and returning war veterans.

The "Tin Can" was demolished in 1977 to make way for Fetzer Gym.

Rufus Hackney was the Tar Heels' leading scorer in 1928 and '29, but UNC met disappointment in the Southern Tournament each season, losing in the early rounds.

nickname was used occasionally for UNC's basketball team well into the 1940s.

TAR HEELS QUIZ

2. What Charlotte family provided the Tar Heels with four players, each of whom was a Carolina captain?

SOUTHERN CONFERENCE DIVIDES Duke's admission into the Southern Conference in 1928 brought the league membership to 23 schools, fueling arguments that the conference was too big and too diverse to be effective.

Finally, in December 1932, a mutually agreeable division was hammered out, and 13 schools, including current ACC member Georgia Tech, withdrew from the Southern Conference to form the Southeastern Conference. North Carolina, N.C. State, Duke, Clemson, Virginia and Maryland, along with South Carolina, VMI, Virginia Tech and Washington & Lee, remained in the Southern Conference.

The 10 Southern Conference schools set a maximum membership at 16 and added Wake Forest, Davidson, William & Mary, Richmond, Furman and The Citadel in 1936 to reach the limit.

That group remained unchanged — except for

Virginia, which withdrew in 1937 and was replaced four years later by George Washington — until the formation of the Atlantic Coast Conference in 1953.

QUEEN CITY TALENT George "Bo" Shepard, the younger brother of Norman Shepard who took over coaching duties of the Tar Heel program following the 1931 season, not only knew his basketball, he also knew basketball talent. He recruited heavily in the Charlotte area, which still had the strongest YMCA and high school programs in the state.

That effort produced players like Virgil Weathers, Stewart Aitken and the McCachrens — Dave, Jim, Bill and George, all of whom played for and captained Tar Heel teams in the '30s and '40s.

Shepard's first team was led by Wilmer Hines and Charlotte products Tom Alexander, Virgil Weathers and Dave McCachren. With a 16-5 record, it was the most exciting Tar Heel team in years.

Tom Alexander, another of Charlotte's contributions to UNC basketball, was a three-year starter. He was the Tar Heels' captain in 1932.

Coached by George "Bo" Shepard, the 1934 team went 18-4 and tied for second place in the Southern Conference, its best finish since 1929. Team members were (front row, left to right) Dave McCachren, Jim McCachren, Jack Glace, Virgil Weathers, Melvin Nelson, (back row) Coach "Bo" Shepard, Ernest Blood, William Beale, Stewart Aitken, Morris Long and team manager Tom Spencer.

In the Southern Conference Tournament, which was being held in Raleigh for the first time, the Tar Heels faced top-seeded Kentucky in the second round. They trailed the heavily favored Wildcats by a point with less than a minute left when Weathers stole a Kentucky pass and drove for a basket to give UNC a 43-42 upset.

The Heels reached the Southern Conference final before losing to Georgia, 26-24.

GLACE AS IN ACE One weakness of Shepard's first team was a lack of height, which was very important in the days when a jump ball followed every basket. The inventive coach found a solution to his problem in 6-foot-4 Ivan "Jack" Glace.

Glace, an excellent student from Harrisburg, Pa., did not play basketball in high school. He came to UNC at the insistence of the dean of the School of Engineering, who was a good friend of Glace's father. Problem was, Glace was so awkward he could hardly walk.

In his first freshman game, Glace tripped and fell as he ran onto the floor to check in with the referee.

"He was so awkward," Shepard said, "… but he wanted to play basketball so badly, he didn't know what to do."

Glace played sparingly as a sophomore. In 1933-34, Glace won a starting job and became a major contributor, helping Carolina go 18-4 and reach the Southern Conference semifinals. Then in 1934-35, he made All-Southern Conference while leading UNC to a 23-2 mark.

1934-35: AT LAST, ANOTHER TITLE

With Aitken, Glace, Jim McCachren and Nelson all returning, joined by Paul Kaveny, the Heels had the makings of their best team in more than a decade.

And that's exactly how it played out. Except for a six-point loss at Duke and a loss at Army, Carolina rolled through the regular season.

The Tar Heels entered the tournament with a 20-2 record. In Raleigh, they rolled over South Carolina (46-25), slipped by N.C. State (30-28), then downed Washington & Lee (35-27) to win their first conference title since 1926.

SHEPARD'S LEGACY "Bo" Shepard's youthful appearance — he often was mistaken for one of his players — and his efficiency as a planner and tactician belied a fiery competitive drive. After four seasons, and a 69-16 record, his health deteriorated, and he was forced to resign as head coach.

In four years, Shepard had turned the Carolina basketball program around and brought it to new national prominence. His New York connections — and the team's frequent northern excursions— caught the eye of promoters.

As a coach, Shepard probably was far ahead of his time. He emphasized planning, thorough preparation, offensive tactics and the importance of good defense — keys to Carolina's program to this day.

Shepard left the Carolina basketball program in good shape, poised to become one of the nation's most successful — and most visible — teams. Shepard would return to UNC in 1941 and serve four years as an assistant athletic director, not counting a one-year military stint in 1944.

It was Walter Skidmore, however, who reaped the dividends of Shepard's work as head coach.

Not that Skidmore didn't contribute to the Tar Heels' success. In fact, Skidmore, in some ways, already had made a contribution. As a high school coach in Charlotte, he sent several of his players to Carolina, including Jim and Bill McCachren, and Stewart Aitken.

The burly Skidmore joined the UNC program as freshman coach in 1934 and posted a 22-1 record in two seasons. He was the logical choice to become varsity coach after health problems forced Shepard's resignation.

Skidmore's first team, in 1935-36, included Jim McCachren, Pete Mullis and Earl Ruth, all of whom had played for him in Charlotte.

TARZAN The 1935-36 team completed the regular season 18-4, losing only to Washington & Lee, to NYU (at

TAR HEELS QUIZ

3. Where did the Tar Heels play their first NCAA postseason game?

In 1939-40, a rule was instituted that gave teams the choice of shooting a free throw or taking the ball out of bounds at midcourt after a foul. On two-shot fouls, the option was applied to the second free throw. UNC used this rule often — as did opponents— to retain ball possession in close games. The rule was eliminated before the 1952-53 season.

TAR HEELS?

University of North Carolina athletic teams have been known as the "Tar Heels" since the beginning, but there's some disagreement about how and when the term "Tar Heel State" originated.

Tar and turpentine, derived from the state's pine forests and used in shipbuilding, were the state's major industrial products in early colonial times. One story has it that, during an invasion of eastern North Carolina by troops under British General Cornwallis during the Revolutionary War, residents dumped tar into the Tar River near Rocky Mount to slow the British crossing. British soldiers observed afterward that anyone attempting to fight in Carolina would have "tar on their heels."

A more likely explanation comes from the Civil War, although there are several different versions of the story.

The best documented version, drawn from a letter by Major Joseph Engelhard, recounts fighting around Petersburg, Va., in the late summer of 1864. As Union forces launched a vicious attack on Confederate positions, several Southern regiments faltered, turned and ran. But a North Carolina regiment, in the center of the battle line, stood fast and repelled the assault.

When Gen. Robert E. Lee heard of the North Carolinians' heroic stand, he remarked, "God bless the Tar Heel boys."

The name, like the tar, stuck.

N.C. COLLECTION, UNC LIBRARY

Andy Bershak was a Tar Heel regular in 1936, '37 and '38, earning second-team All-SC Tournament honors in 1936 and '37. He also played end on Carolina's football teams, earning All-America awards in 1936 and '37.

Madison Square Garden, when Ruth missed the game because of an injury) and to Virginia and Duke in overtime. North Carolina finished second in the conference behind W&L, led by 6-foot-6 Bob Spessard.

In the league tournament, Carolina easily handled Virginia (39-21) in the first round, then beat State, 31-28. The first half of the title game, however, was all Washington & Lee. Led by Spessard, the Generals held a commanding 31-19 lead at intermission.

As the Tar Heels warmed up for the second half, a large, rather imposing figure made its way from the Raleigh Auditorium stands and onto the court. He shook hands with each UNC player, then ambled to the center circle and let loose a long, loud whoop that shook the auditorium's rafters. There was no mistaking Lath Morris, a Farmville, N.C., resident whose vociferous support at Tar Heel football games had earned him nicknames such as "Tarzan" and "The Screaming Eagle."

Morris launched into a version of "Hark The Sound," and when he finished, he turned toward the Washington & Lee team, which now was doubled over in laughter, and proceeded to place a "hex" on the Carolina opponents.

Whether it was Morris' hex or the Tar Heels' talent,

Carolina chipped away at the W&L lead in the second half and staged a furious rally late in the game to win the championship.

"The defending title holders, trailing by a dozen points at the half — 31 to 19 — and by as much as 11 points midway of the final period, produced a stirring rally to count 19 points in the stretch while limiting the Generals to three points, all on free throws," Anthony J. McKevlin wrote in *The News & Observer*. "The top-seeded Generals, a grand ball club, were beaten by a team which rose to the heights to offer one of the greatest comebacks in North Carolina sports history."

Morris made his way back to the court during the postgame awards ceremonies. North Carolina Governor J.C.B. Ehringhaus, in presenting the trophy to the champions, offered that, perhaps, Morris should get an award, too. The Governor and "Tarzan" shook hands on it.

SKIDMORE HITS SKIDS Unfortunately, Skidmore — and the Tar Heels — were unable to recapture the magic of 1936 in subsequent seasons. After several mediocre seasons, the final straw came with a 10-11 record in 1938-39. It was UNC's first losing mark since 1920, and Skidmore stepped down as head coach.

THE BLIND BOMBER George Glamack was Wallace Wade's gift to the University of North Carolina.

Glamack was a football and basketball star in his hometown of Johnstown, Pa., and although a football injury had left him almost completely blind in his left eye, he was eagerly sought by many colleges along the East Coast that had football and basketball programs.

Walter Skidmore's 1937 Tar Heels battled through injuries to finish second in the Southern Conference with an 18-5 record. The team included (front row, left to right) John Stoopack, Fred Little, Andy Bershak, Earl Ruth, Bill McCachren, Pete Mullis, (back row) Coach Skidmore, David Meroney, Pete Boone, Henry Wright, Ramsay Potts, Foy Grubb and team manager Ernest McKee.

Glamack chose Duke, where he hoped to play under Wade, the Blue Devils' legendary football coach. Once there, though, Glamack didn't take to Wade's coaching, so he moved down the road to UNC, where he decided to play basketball instead.

Glamack played as a sophomore on Skidmore's last team in 1938-39. It wasn't until the 1939-40 season, after football assistant coach Bill Lange had become head basketball coach, that Glamack emerged as the undisputed star of his era.

Two factors contributed to Glamack's success. One was the addition to the 1939-40 team of exceptional passers in Bob Rose, Bobby Gersten and Jimmy Howard. Rose became Glamack's "eyes" on the court.

"Rose knew just how to pass the ball to me with a lead, so I had about a step and a half or two ahead of the defensive man," Glamack explained. "They could never stop the shot. We worked on this play all the time in practice. Rose had a way of passing into the pivot that no one I've seen since could do."

George Glamack, the Tar Heels' "Blind Bomber," led Carolina to its first NCAA postseason appearance in 1940. He set a UNC and SC record with a 45-point performance against Clemson in 1941 and was Helms Foundation Player of the Year in 1940 and 1941.

The second factor was Glamack himself. He couldn't see the basket, could hardly see the backboard, but he devised his own scheme for judging the position and distance to the goal by looking at the markings on the floor.

"I designed a Braille system all my own watching the black lines on the floor near the basket," he said. "I just got my spot on the floor and shot from there. I took a long time to develop it, but I developed it."

Glamack stood 6-foot-6. Playing down low, with his back to the basket, he could roll either way and shoot the hook shot with either hand. He was unstoppable.

Glamack's prowess on the court and his determination (and success) in overcoming his handicap contributed to his reputation. He took time to work with groups of handicapped people and also taught a youth Sunday school class.

Glamack was a god in Chapel Hill and almost as highly revered everywhere else. In 1940, the King of Yugoslavia (Glamack was born Gjuro Gregorvitch Giamociij and was of Serbian descent) invited him to come to Yugoslavia to introduce basketball to that country, and Glamack planned to do that after graduation from UNC until World War II intervened.

As for Glamack's abilities on the court, in 1940 Duke coach Eddie Cameron was a member of the coaches' All-America committee and was asked to submit five names for the All-America team. Cameron wrote down only one name — George Glamack.

Jimmy Howard was one of a trio of superb passers who helped the Tar Heels win SC titles in 1940 and 1941.

WOOLLEN GYM

The Indoor Athletic Court — the "Tin Can" — always had been considered a "temporary" structure. As early as 1924, University business manager Charles T. Woollen had urged construction of a permanent basketball facility, which, Woollen reported to the Board of Trustees, would cost about $350,000.

By 1928, the Board's Building Committee had initiated plans for a facility, at an estimated cost of $400,000. It wasn't until 1936, however, that construction plans were finalized. That was when Mr. and Mrs. James E. Millis of High Point offered to contribute all the equipment to furnish a new gymnasium. Bowman Gray, Bowman Gray Jr. and Gordon Gray of Winston-Salem followed with an offer to finance construction of a pool next door to the new gym.

The project, begun in 1937, was completed in 1938. In addition to the pool and gymnasium, the facility included six basketball courts — two for competition, four for practice.

The facility was named the Charles T. Woollen Gymnasium, in honor of the business manager who had urged construction of the building for more than a decade. "Total cost was $646,000," read a 1938 report to the Board of Trustees, "none of which came from state appropriations."

Lange built the 1939-40 team around his nearly blind pivot man, and it paid huge dividends. Glamack averaged almost 14 points a game, and the Tar Heels went 23-3, winning both the Southern Conference regular-season and tournament championships.

Glamack was named a first-team selection on every All-America team and was voted National Player of the Year by the Helms Foundation.

In 1940-41, Glamack was even better. He averaged 20.6 points a game — an unheard-of figure in those days of 40-point games.

N.C. COLLECTION, UNC LIBRARY

Paul Severin, like Andy Bershak before him, was a two-sport star for the Tar Heels. Severin was an All-Southern Conference pick in basketball in 1940 and an All-American end on the football team in '39 and '40.

1940-41: FIRST NCAA TRIP

The Heels went 19-6, again winning the Southern Conference regular-season title. In the first round of the tournament, however, Duke pulled a 38-37 upset.

In those days, however, teams advancing to the NCAA Tournament, first held in 1939, were chosen on a regional basis, with a committee determining the representative from each of eight regions. Carolina was chosen to represent the South in the Eastern Regional playoffs at Madison, Wis.

UNC's first venture into NCAA play was a disaster. In the first round against Pittsburgh, Carolina hit nine of 65 shots — Pitt went nine for 69. Glamack picked up two quick fouls, and then fouled out with three minutes left. He scored nine points. The Heels led 12-8 at halftime, but Pitt scored nine straight points to start the second half (with Glamack on the bench) and held on to win, 26-20.

The Tar Heels played much better the following night in the consolation game, but could not stop Dartmouth's huge front line of Jim Olsen, Gustave Broberg and George Munroe, all of whom stood taller than 6-foot-4. The teams

GEORGE GLAMACK'S LEGACY

George Glamack was a star of his era and the equal of future Basketball Hall of Fame performers Hank Liusetti, a scoring star at Stanford in the late 1930s, and DePaul's George Mikan, considered the game's first great big man in the mid-1940s.

NORTH CAROLINA COLLECTION, UNIVERSITY OF NORTH CAROLINA LIBRARY AT CHAPEL HILL

"Blind Bomber" George Glamack tosses up his famous hook shot in the Tar Heels' 53-49 loss to NYU in the Tin Can on Jan. 18, 1941. Glamack scored 22 of Carolina's 49 points that night.

After his graduation from UNC in 1941, Glamack played for a number of professional teams and was a major attraction wherever he played, often drawing sell-out crowds to the small (by today's standards) arenas in Akron, Buffalo, Newark and other stops on the pro circuit.

He volunteered for military duty during World War II and, despite his poor eyesight, served in the U.S. Navy, most of his tour at the Great Lakes Naval Air Station.

The pre-induction physical included the obligatory eye chart, and as Glamack later related the story, he told the doctors he couldn't see the letters, and in fact, couldn't see the chart. The doctors told him to move closer.

"I got to the wall, and I bumped into it," Glamack said. "The doctor told me that wasn't bad at all and I was a sailor."

Glamack's pro career was cut short by arthritis, and he later spent almost a year in a veterans' hospital in Buffalo, N.Y. Although told at one point he would never walk again, the former Tar Heel had overcome obstacles throughout his life and was walking again within a year.

Glamack died in the early 1980s.

George Glamack (left), Bobby Rose (center) and Hank Pessar (right) chase a loose ball during a victory over Duke in the 1941 season.

set a Wisconsin Field House record of 119 total points (60-59 Wisconsin), with Glamack scoring 31.

Glamack again was named a first-team All-American and again was chosen National Player of the Year by the Helms Foundation.

LANGE DEPARTS Bill Lange resigned because of illness after the 1944 season. His five-year record was a respectable 85-41, but over the last two years of his tenure, he suffered from debilitating migraine headaches.

Luckily for UNC, another coach was waiting in the wings. Ben Carnevale was a star at New York University and had been assigned to Carolina as a lieutenant in the Navy ROTC program. He began his coaching career with intramural and club teams around Chapel Hill and was tabbed for the varsity job after Lange resigned.

Carnevale, only a year or so older than his players at the time, stayed just two seasons, but they were an eventful two years.

In Carnevale's first season, UNC finished 22-6 and beat N.C. State, South Carolina and Duke to win the Southern Conference Tournament. It was the Tar Heels' first tournament crown since 1940.

Carolina received bids to the NCAA Tournament and the National Invitation Tournament in New York, but could not play because wartime restrictions limited travel by the Navy personnel on the team, including Coach Carnevale.

The Tar Heels had four starters — John Dillon, Bob Paxton, Jim Jordan and Don Anderson — back for the 1945-46 season. And to that quartet, Carnevale added guards Jim White (back from military duty) and Taylor Thorne, forward Red Hughes … and Bones McKinney.

George "Blind Bomber" Glamack was fitted for contact lenses in 1940 and was one of the first athletes to wear them. The lenses were designed at Duke, supposedly made in Switzerland and cost $1,000, with UNC picking up the tab. Unfortunately, the lenses were big (as large as an eyeball, Glamack said) and uncomfortable. He could keep them in no longer than 10 minutes at a time, and as a result, Glamack never wore them during games.

George "Toad" McCachren (left) and Jim McCachren look over some of the Tar Heels' basketball hardware during the war-time 1943 season. George was the Heels' captain in '43, Jim in 1936. Two other McCachren brothers were also Tar Heel captains — Dave in 1934 and Bill in 1939.

Basketball rules were amended in 1910 to disqualify a player after his fourth personal foul. Before that, there was no foul limit, although a player could be disqualified, and no substitution for him allowed, if he fouled "with the evident intent to injure" his opponent. In 1942, the rule was amended to allow players eligible to start an overtime an extra (fifth) foul in the overtime period. For the 1944-45 season, the "bonus" foul was eliminated in favor of a five-foul limit.

BONES North Carolina's athletic program — in fact, all the programs of the Southern and Atlantic Coast conferences — has never produced a character to rival Horace Albert McKinney.

McKinney is claimed — or maybe disclaimed — by three of the state's "Big Four" universities and has a childhood connection to the fourth. He was born in Lowland, N.C., in the Pamlico County marshlands of eastern North Carolina, grew up in Durham near the Duke University campus, played two seasons at N.C. State, returned from the Army to play part of one season at Carolina, and then spent 13 seasons at Wake Forest, the last eight as the Demon Deacons' head coach.

McKinney both played and coached in the NCAA Final Four, was one of the founding fathers (as a player and coach) of the National Basketball Association, became a Baptist preacher, coached the state's first professional basketball team (the ABA Carolina Cougars) and was among the pioneer broadcasters for the ACC basketball television network.

And "Bones," a nickname he acquired after playing "Beau Brummel Bones" in a grade-school production, kept teammates, coaches and fans laughing the whole time.

McKinney, 6-foot-6, was released from the Army in early January 1946. He had been a star on the great Durham High teams that won 75 straight games from 1937-40, starred on N.C. State's freshman team in '41, led the Southern Conference in scoring for coach Bob

Warren's Wolfpack varsity in '42 and had his jersey No. 5 retired by Fort Bragg. He was an exceptionally smart and talented pivotman. He also was a clown and a cut-up.

McKinney's reputation was established in high school and built through his years at State and in the military. He harassed referees unmercifully, talked to opponents and joked with fans. In lopsided games, he would take a seat in the stands, leaving his four teammates to play four-on-five. He'd score a goal, then on his way downcourt, stop by the scorer's table to make certain he was credited with the two points.

By the time he was released by the Army, McKinney was 26 years old and had a wife and a son, the first of his six children. He also had educational benefits under the GI Bill.

Coach Bob Warren, however, left N.C. State in 1942, and McKinney elected not to return to Raleigh. He met Carnevale when UNC had played Fort Bragg and became good friends with the Carolina coach, who was two years his senior.

1945-46: TO THE FINAL FOUR

Ben Carnevale was barely older than his players when he became UNC's coach in 1944.

On Jan. 9, 1946, Bones McKinney became a Tar Heel. He didn't play until Jan. 15 (he scored six points, Jim Jordan had 17 and John Dillon 11 in a 58-30 rout at Davidson), and by then, the Tar Heels were well into their season. Their record stood at 12-2 with the only losses to a military outfit from Greensboro, 64-63, on Dec. 11, and to Duke, 51-46 in overtime the same day McKinney enrolled at UNC.

With McKinney replacing Don Anderson at center, the Tar Heels won 17 straight. Little Creek Air Base ended the win streak, 60-46, on Feb. 23. McKinney had been admitted to the student infirmary the day before suffering from a severe cold and upset stomach while Dillon had been hospitalized that morning with an infected arm resulting from a deep bruise inflicted in the previous game. Neither made the trip.

The team averaged almost 56 points a game, an astronomical total for the time, and set a school record by scoring 1,647 points during the regular season.

Carolina was 27-3 and heavily favored going into the Southern Conference Tournament, which was being played for the last time in Raleigh Memorial Auditorium. In '47, the event moved to the 8,000-seat Duke Indoor Stadium, now Cameron Indoor Stadium.

The Tar Heels easily dispatched Maryland in the first round, 54-27. In the semifinals against Wake Forest, however, the Carolina shooters went cold and the Tar Heels lost to the Deacons, 31-29.

Jim Jordan was one of four starters returning for the 1945-46 season, which saw the Heels advance to the Final Four.

Duke went on to win the tournament, but the three-man NCAA district committee — chaired by former UNC coach Norman Shepard and including Gus Tebell of Virginia and Adolph Rupp of Kentucky — bypassed the Blue Devils and picked Carolina to be the region's representative to the NCAA East Regionals in Madison Square Garden.

THE EAST REGIONAL In New York, the Tar Heels almost repeated their debacle of 1941, when they lost in the first round.

Dillon struggled early, but when he picked up his game so did the rest of the Carolina team, which went on to beat NYU, 57-49.

In the regional finals the next night, the Tar Heels faced a strong Ohio State team led by 6-foot-6 Jack Underman. Bob Paxton hit a long one-hander with 20 seconds left to tie the score 54-54 and send the game into overtime, then the Heels held on to pull out a 60-57 victory and a berth in the national championship game against Oklahoma A&M and its 7-foot star, Bob Kurland.

AWESOME AGGIES Most of the Tar Heels had never seen a 7-foot player, and Kurland was an imposing sight. Sam

Bones McKinney (with the ball) kept North Carolina in the 1946 championship game against the Oklahoma A&M Aggies. But once McKinney fouled out, the Heels were done.

Aubrey, 6-foot-4 ½, and 6-foot-1 Blake Williams were
the forwards, and one of the guards was 6-foot-1 A.L.
Bennett. The Aggies were monstrous by the standards of
those days.

Plus, Oklahoma A&M was coached by the legendary
Henry Iba. The Aggies had won the title the year before,
and they were 28-2 entering the postseason tournament.

During the championship game, McKinney bombarded
Kurland with words, talking him to distraction.

"All-American?" McKinney said as the two centers
stood side-by-side on the floor. "You're not even All-
Madison Square Garden."

Dillon, meanwhile, was throwing down hook shots —
he scored 16 points before fouling out with about 20

UNC AND WORLD WAR II

For a handful of schools,
including UNC, World War II provided a bonanza of athletic talent.

Of course, the war-time draft
took a big bite out of the male
college-age population. War-time
restrictions on travel and use of
essential materials like gasoline
and tires disrupted scheduling.
Some schools abandoned
intercollegiate athletics entirely
during the period.

But, the military also made good
use of college educational facilities
during the war. The Navy, in
particular, elected to utilize college
facilities for pre-flight training for
its aviators and designated eight
universities as sites for these Naval
Aviation Physical Training
Programs, called V-5 in military
parlance. Carolina's modern
athletic facilities (Woollen Gym
and Bowman Gray Pool), the
availability of housing (the "Tin
Can" was converted to barracks)
and Chapel Hill's proximity to
major military installations led to
UNC being chosen as one of the
two V-5 sites in the South. The
University of Georgia was the other.

The Pre-Flight School and a

similar V-12 program for Naval
reserve officers brought more than
1,500 young men to the UNC
campus. And, even better for
UNC, the Navy required that
competitive athletics be part of the
officers' training. These programs
contributed dozens of athletes to
Tar Heel teams, including Jim
Jordan, a second-team basketball
All-American in 1945.

The military also provided
competition. Most military bases
had athletic teams, and these
teams, many featuring former or
later-to-be college and pro stars,
were able, willing opponents for
area college teams. Fort Bragg's
team, which played UNC for
several seasons, included Bones
McKinney, who later led the Tar
Heels to the 1946 Final Four,
former N.C. State captain Ray
Smith and future pro players Odie
Spears, Walter "Tea Pot" Frye,
Hugh Hampton and Carl Snow.

When the war ended,
thousands of young war-time
veterans, with GI educational
benefits in hand, returned home,
creating another bonanza for
college athletic programs.

seconds left — and Carolina kept it close against heavily favored A&M.

But it couldn't last. About five minutes into the second half, McKinney was whistled for his fourth personal foul. McKinney fouled out with 9:06 left in the game.

Without Bones to annoy him, Kurland dominated the final minutes. He scored the Aggies' last nine points,

"HOOK" DILLON

John "Hook" Dillon might be the ultimate rags-to-riches-to-rags story.

Dillon had been a star at Benedictine (Ga.) Military Academy, but like many young men of the time, couldn't afford college and spent several years working for the Savannah Ice Delivery Co. and playing for the company's city league basketball team. He had enrolled at Georgia Tech in 1945 when Ben Carnevale, the new basketball coach at Carolina, wrote to ask if he'd been interested in coming to Chapel Hill.

Carnevale worked out the details, and Dillon came to Carolina, where his uncannily accurate hook shots made him an immediate hit. Teaming with Navy ROTC veteran Jim Jordan, he averaged 7.3 points and helped lead the Tar Heels to a 22-6 record.

The following year, with military vets Jim White and Bones McKinney joining the lineup, the Heels went 30-5, reaching the NCAA Championship game. Dillon averaged almost 15 points a game and was chosen an All-American.

So famous was his hook shot that, on the eve of the 1946 championship game against Oklahoma A&M, Dillon, a devout Catholic, was invited to meet New York's Cardinal Spellman. "No introduction is necessary," the Cardinal said as the two met. "I know 'The Hook.'"

But Dillon was a true, one-dimensional player. Carnevale left UNC the next year, as did McKinney, Jordan and much of the Tar Heel talent. Without those players around him, Dillon couldn't carry the load.

"Hook couldn't play defense, couldn't pass the ball, couldn't rebound," said McKinney, Dillon's best friend. "He only knew how to do two things: Shoot a hook shot and win."

New coach Tom Scott found it hard to bench an All-American, and he kept Dillon in the lineup. But by February 1947, the Heels were 9-7 and in danger of missing the Southern Conference Tournament, and Scott replaced Dillon with Nemo Nearman, a 6-foot-7 freshman from West Virginia. The Tar Heels won their last 10 games before losing to N.C. State in the Southern Conference final.

Dillon, a consensus second-team All-American as a sophomore, spent part of his junior year and all of his senior year in 1947-48 as a reserve.

"Dillon was a real nice kid," Scott recalled later. "He just accepted the change and never stopped playing his heart out."

finishing with 23 before fouling out with 34 seconds remaining, and Oklahoma A&M pulled away to win, 43-40.

POST BONES McKinney left UNC shortly after the end of the '46 season, taking a job with Hanes Hosiery Co. in Winston-Salem to support his growing family. In less than a year, he was back in basketball, playing and later coaching for the Washington Capitols in the new Basketball Association of America, later to be the NBA.

Soon, Carnevale was gone, too. His record at UNC — 52-11 in two seasons — caught the attention of the Navy, and the brilliant young coach was offered what amounted to a lifetime contract to coach at the U.S. Naval Academy.

With large numbers of young men leaving the military, there were plenty of candidates to replace Carnevale. UNC picked Tom Scott, a Navy veteran from Kansas who had been a semi-pro star and had coached at Concordia (Minn.) College and Missouri State Teachers College before the war.

Scott's record was impressive — he had won four conference titles in five years at MSTC — but for Carolina, he was the wrong man in the wrong place at the wrong time.

EVERETT CASE Unfortunately for Scott and for UNC, Scott's first season coincided with Everett Case's first season at N.C. State.

Case, Indiana born and bred, was hired to build a competitive program in Raleigh, and he did that and much more. His Wolfpack teams dominated the late 1940s and early '50s, winning six straight Southern Conference Tournament championships. In 1949, Case instituted the Dixie Classic, a showcase for college basketball that outshone even the NCAA and NIT playoffs until its demise in the aftermath of the gambling scandals of the late '50s and early '60s.

For more than a decade, Case and N.C. State set the standard for college basketball in the South, and everyone else had to scramble to keep pace.

SIX YEARS OF FRUSTRATION Scott's teams won 100 games and lost 65 in his six seasons as head coach. Still, the Tar Heels were continually frustrated by N.C. State.

Scott's teams lost 15 straight games to Case's Wolfpack. After beating the Heels in the '47 Southern Conference championship, the Wolfpack also knocked UNC out of the Southern playoffs in 1948 and 1949.

In 1950-51 and '51-52, the Tar Heels hit bottom, going 12-15 both seasons and failing to qualify for the Southern Conference Tournament. Scott resigned after the 1951-52 season.

After UNC's appearance in the '46 NCAA championship, the team dispersed from New York for spring break. Many of the players went home, not back to Chapel Hill, precluding any welcome-home celebration. Carnevale, whose Navy hitch was almost up and who had not been offered the Carolina job permanently, stayed in New York to visit with his family. Reportedly, he was a candidate for several coaching jobs, including ones at Cornell and Harvard, and was not expected to return to UNC. He was offered the Navy job the following summer.

Tom Scott guided the Tar Heels to the Southern Conference finals in 1947, but couldn't match that success in four succeeding seasons.

1952-61:
Frank McGuire Era

Embarrassed by the losing records of the past two seasons, frustrated by 15 straight losses to Everett Case's Wolfpack teams and with the recriminations against "big-time" athletics in the wake of the gambling scandals quickly fading, North Carolina was looking for a successful coach after the 1951-52 season, someone who could beat N.C. State and put the Tar Heels back among the nation's elite.

Around Chapel Hill and the state, one name quickly came to the forefront — Frank McGuire.

McGuire, a native New Yorker, had coached St. John's to the NCAA championship game the year before and had been named national Coach of the Year. He was well-known and extremely popular in Chapel Hill, having spent part of his World War II tour in the Navy V-5 program at UNC.

A strong recommendation by Ben Carnevale clinched it. Athletic Director Chuck Erickson offered McGuire the job, and he quickly accepted.

New York-style basketball was coming to Tobacco Road.

UNC Athletic Director Chuck Erickson (center) and Coach Frank McGuire (right) welcomed aboard new assistant coach Dean Smith in 1958.

ROOTS Frank McGuire was born and raised in Brooklyn, and his father was a New York City policeman. He starred in basketball, baseball and football at St. Francis Xavier High School, and then attended St. John's University, just a few blocks from his home. He started for four seasons in basketball and baseball and captained both Redmen teams as a senior.

Frank McGuire, a New York native, had coached St. John's to the NCAA championship game in both basketball and baseball before taking over the Tar Heels in 1952-53.

After graduating from St. John's, McGuire became head basketball coach at Xavier High, compiling a 126-39 record from 1936 to 1947. In '47, he returned to St. John's to coach the basketball and baseball teams.

Except for two years in the Navy during World War II — part of that in Chapel Hill — McGuire had spent his whole life in the City.

McGuire's abilities as a coach were unquestioned. His record at Xavier proved that. At St. John's, he rebuilt a sagging program in two years, winning 24 games in his third season and taking the Redmen to the NCAA Championship (where they lost to Kansas) two years later. His five-year record at St. John's was 106-37.

Above all, McGuire was a charmer. Loquacious and polite, he made friends wherever he went, and once you became a friend of Frank McGuire's, you remained a friend for life.

McGuire fell in love with Chapel Hill when he was assigned there during the war. He liked the small-town, intimate college atmosphere, so different from the bustle of New York, and thought it would be a wonderful place to raise a family. He also liked the challenge of rebuilding Carolina's program.

When offered the job, McGuire listed only one demand. He wanted Buck Freeman, his old coach at St. John's, as his assistant. Freeman was unemployed and had fallen on hard times. Frank McGuire never forgot a friend.

Freeman remained on UNC's staff until 1958, when failing health forced his retirement. He was replaced by an unknown young assistant from the Air Force Academy named Dean Smith.

RECRUITING N.Y. STYLE McGuire once said he had everyone in New York recruiting for him. That almost was true.

Buck Freeman coached Frank McGuire at St. John's, then McGuire asked to bring Freeman along when he came to Chapel Hill.

The inner city contained a labyrinth of municipal playgrounds, dimly lit gyms, public-school courts and run-down youth centers that attracted not only the city's best basketball players, but also a handful of shady characters who served as "talent scouts."

McGuire knew them all. They were his friends, and McGuire never had a better friend than Harry Gotkin.

Gotkin, a stocky, balding man in his early 50s, owned a small manufacturing firm in the garment district, and his brother Java had been a teammate of McGuire's at St. John's. Gotkin was proud of New York and the basketball talent the city produced. And he was proud of his friendship with McGuire and wanted to see his friend do well at North Carolina.

Being a "talent scout" in New York City was a dog-eat-dog business, too. It didn't hurt that Gotkin's chief competitor was Howie Garfinkel, who scouted for N.C. State.

Gotkin was a tireless worker on McGuire's behalf. He was also smooth, an excellent judge of talent and an even better judge of people.

"One advantage I had over the other scouts," Gotkin explained in *Tar Heel*, "is that I didn't pester kids all hours of the night. Some of the others did. I let the others do their talking first. Then I moved in. Nine times out of 10 the kid wound up where I wanted him."

The silky-tongued Gotkin — "Uncle Harry" to his boys — did the leg work, then McGuire or one of his assistant coaches finished it off.

Dean Smith recalled his first meeting with Gotkin in Thad Mumau's *Dean Smith: A Biography*:

"I arrived up there in April 1959. Harry met me at the airport and said, 'Let's go over here and see this team.' He said, 'We've got this player and this one,' and he named off five players. The five were Art Heyman, Larry Brown, Dick Brennan, Kenny McIntyre and Billy Galantai. Harry added, 'All five are set. They're going to Carolina.' I said, 'Great, Harry,' and that was the recruiting trip."

Brown and Galantai wound up at UNC. Brennan and McIntyre later attended prep school in North Carolina but never made it to Chapel Hill. Heyman became an All-American at Duke.

Many of the "scouts" were paid for channeling players to certain colleges, a violation of NCAA rules, but Gotkin vowed he never got a cent from McGuire or UNC. McGuire said the same.

"No one gets paid, but everybody looks out for me," McGuire said. "The whole police department looks for players for me. So do the high school coaches and so do the brothers at the Catholic schools. Even the waterfront looks out for me.

"No one gets paid. Gotkin doesn't get paid. He looks out for me because he's a friend of mine. Why shouldn't I get the New York players? After all, that's my home territory."

ALL ABOARD McGuire needed four years to get his program on track at UNC. Tom Scott had left the cupboard pretty bare, although players like Vince Grimaldi, Jack Wallace, Al Lifson, Ernie Schwartz and

Some accounts place an emphasis on Frank McGuire's concern for his son Frankie, who had cerebral palsy, when discussing McGuire's decision to come to North Carolina. Those evaluations argue that McGuire's decision was influenced by the presence of excellent medical facilities at UNC and Duke and his desire to move his son into a less-hurried, more-hospitable environment. McGuire said in later interviews that Frankie's welfare was a factor, but not an overwhelming one, since he was getting excellent medical care in New York.

Paul Likins kept the team from being a total washout.

In 1952-53, McGuire added the first of his New York recruits — Jerry Vayda, Gerry McCabe and Bud Maddie, a transfer. Two more New Yorkers — Tony Radovich and Gene Glancy — joined at midseason.

Despite a spate of injuries, the Tar Heels finished a respectable 17-10. On Jan. 24, 1953, they accomplished what many thought impossible — they beat N.C. State.

In an interview two months earlier, McGuire said, "State's in a different class. We don't hope to beat them until the 1954-55 season. We'll be ready for teams like State then."

But the Tar Heels hung in before a crazed crowd of 12,400 in Reynolds Coliseum, and then with 26 seconds left, Vayda hit a jump shot from the right side to put Carolina ahead, 70-69. State brought the ball in, but then lost possession when a player dribbled the ball off his foot and it went out of bounds. Lifson dribbled away the last seconds, and when the horn sounded, "Coach McGuire was hoisted to the shoulders of his happy warriors and went through the ceremony of cutting

TAR HEELS QUIZ

4. Which former Tar Heel, a reserve on the 1917 team, later broke a chandelier in the Governor's Mansion with an errant basketball pass?

Al Lifson, the leading scorer on Tom Scott's 1952 team, was a solid performer for Frank McGuire in 1953, '54 and '55.

down the nets… ," said a report in *The News & Observer*.

Carolina later lost to Case's Wolfpack in Chapel Hill (87-66) and in the first round of the Southern Conference Tournament (86-54), when the Heels hit 17 of 69 shots. Nonetheless, McGuire's "Underground Railroad" was up and running and gathering steam.

THANKS, MOM As the ACC was born in Greensboro, Harry Gotkin was reeling in his first big catch — no doubt, his biggest catch — for Frank McGuire.

Several years earlier, during a New York City teachers' strike, Buck Freeman had worked with Lennie Rosenbluth, then a rising sophomore at James Monroe High School. Freeman urged McGuire to give the promising youngster a look.

Gotkin caught up with Rosenbluth later that same year and nursed the young prospect through his last two seasons at Monroe.

Gotkin convinced Rosenbluth's mother that her son should go to Carolina and play for McGuire, but Rosenbluth's grades weren't good enough to get him

TAR HEELS QUIZ

5. Who, according to the best records available, were the first brothers to play on the same UNC team?

THE ATLANTIC COAST CONFERENCE

In May 1953, the face of Southern basketball changed dramatically.

Officials of the 17 Southern Conference schools met in Greensboro to iron out problems involving football bowl participation and freshman eligibility. Maryland and Clemson had been suspended in 1952 for participating in bowl games in violation of the Southern Conference ban on postseason games, a policy that had been waived on numerous occasions. Freshman eligibility had been off-and-on; the ban on use of freshmen had been suspended during the war years, reinstated in 1948, then suspended again during the Korean War in 1951-52.

Neither issue was resolved, but on the night of May 7, representatives from seven of the conference schools met separately and drew up a plan for a new conference. UNC's representatives at the meeting were Chancellor Robert B. House; Dr. Allan W. Hobbs, the faculty chairman of athletics; Athletic Director Chuck Erickson; and Dr. Oliver K. Cornwell, chairman of the Department of Physical Education and Athletics.

The plan was presented to the full Southern Conference membership the next day, with Dr. James T. Penney, faculty chairman at South Carolina and chairman of the splinter group's committee, emphasizing that the division was undertaken "with mixed feelings" and that the seven schools retained "certain obligations

High-scoring Lennie Rosenbluth was the apple of Coach Frank McGuire's eye and the hero for Tar Heel fans in 1956-57.

and commitments which we in no way wish to abrogate."

By late that evening, the division of the Southern Conference had been accomplished. The seven schools — UNC, N.C. State, Duke, Wake Forest, Clemson, South Carolina and Maryland — agreed to meet in Raleigh in June to iron out details for the 1952-53 school year. An eighth school — Virginia — joined the group in December.

"The splitting of the Southern Conference, although not unexpected, came suddenly," Wilton Garrison of *The Charlotte Observer* wrote. "… The new group has the good wishes and blessing of the old. Several of the new members said they would not join unless they had the approval of their good friends which they got.

"Both the new and old conferences have fine opportunities ahead of them. There are many problems to settle … but it is an opportunity to have two strong leagues (according to their own strength) due to better matching and more equality. … Here's wishing good luck to both."

The new conference didn't get a name until the June meeting in Raleigh.

In the interim, newspapers throughout the region had suggested names like Shoreline, Confederate, East Coast, Blue-Gray, Dixie, Rebel, Seaboard, Colonial, Mid-Atlantic, Mid-South, Tobacco, Cotton, Big 8, Southern Seven and Piedmont.

Duke's Eddie Cameron suggested Atlantic Coast. Logically, Cameron said, all seven schools are in states bordering the Atlantic. And on the opposite side of the continent, there already was a Pacific Coast Conference. The name was unanimously approved.

admitted. Gotkin was so convincing, however, that Mrs. Rosenbluth sold some of her furs to pay her son's tuition— about $800 — to Staunton Military Academy in Virginia, where Rosenbluth earned the grades he needed.

Rosenbluth's play at Staunton Military also caught the eye of dozens of other colleges. When it came time to choose a school, Mrs. Rosenbluth stood firm. She said they had made a promise to Harry Gotkin and would stick to it. Rosenbluth enrolled at Carolina.

LEAN YEARS AT UNC The reinstated ban on freshmen delayed McGuire's rebuilding at Carolina. Vayda and Radovich were sophomores in '54, but the centerpiece of the rebuilding was Rosenbluth, who spent the season on the freshman team.

Oddly, the freshman team struggled, too, despite the presence of Rosenbluth (who scored 41 in a loss to Wake Forest), Bob Young and Joe Quigg. The Tar Babies did hand the State freshman team its only defeat, 61-60, in 19 games that season.

Meanwhile, McGuire's varsity lost three straight in the Dixie Classic — to Navy, Seton Hall and Oregon State — and was beaten three times by Case's Wolfpack, including a 52-51 heartbreaker in the opening round of

TELEVISION & THE TAR HEELS

Over the last decade, television has become a driving force in college basketball. It wasn't always that way, of course. In the early 1950s, television was in its infancy, few games were televised and fans relied on radio and newspapers for results and game reports.

All that began to change in the mid-1950's, when Philadelphia businessman Castleman D. Chesley devised a plan to televise weekly Atlantic Coast Conference games. Chesley's vision grew into the ACC-TV Network, the first regularly scheduled regional college basketball telecasts in the country.

Not surprisingly, North Carolina was the centerpiece. After all, Carolina's program was the most successful and most visible in the

ACC in that period. Still, the Tar Heels' television history goes back further than that.

The first telecast of a college basketball championship game was in 1946, when WCBS-TV in New York arranged a local television broadcast of the NCAA Championship game between the Tar Heels and Oklahoma A&M in Madison Square Garden. The telecast was carried only in the New York City area, but the estimated viewing audience was more than half a million.

On Jan. 8, 1955, the university's fledgling public television station, WUNC, arranged the first telecast of an ACC game — Carolina vs. Wake Forest in Woollen Gym. The television signal could be received the first ACC Tournament, played at Reynolds.

The tournament meeting had ominous overtones. In the first game that year, an 84-77 Wolfpack win at Woollen, McGuire had accused Case of using a full-court press to force a "fouling contest"(UNC committed 38 fouls in the game, still a Carolina record) and to expose the Tar Heels' weak bench. In the second game, a 57-48 Wolfpack win at Reynolds, State held the ball for six minutes and play was delayed in the second quarter when a fan in the upper deck threw a whisky bottle that shattered at midcourt.

The day before the tournament, UNC vice president Billy Carmichael invited McGuire and Case to meet for breakfast at the Carolina Inn, and the two coaches talked for several hours.

"It was all very pleasant," McGuire said later. "Everett and I have differences on quite a few things. … But I think we understand each other better now."

Still, the tournament game was a war.

Brilliant ball handling by Skippy Winstead, a senior from Roxboro, N.C., kept Carolina in the contest, and with 12 seconds left, Gerry McCabe scored to cut State's lead to 51-50. Then Radovich fouled State's Dave Gotkin, and Gotkin threw the ball at Radovich. Radovich was

Bob Young was part of the 1954 recruiting class that became the foundation of Carolina's 1957 national championship team.

only within a 50-mile radius of Chapel Hill, and the game was a sellout. But the Duke-N.C. State game, being played at the same time in Durham, drew 2,000 fewer than capacity, and league and school officials blamed television for the low turnout.

Chesley got involved at the end of the 1957 season. He negotiated a deal, through his station in Wilmington, Del., to telecast UNC's NCAA East Regional semifinal against Canisius, played in The Palestra in Philadelphia. WBTV in Charlotte, WTVD in Durham and WFMY in Greensboro carried the game.

By this time, the NCAA had entered the picture. It had negotiated a deal, beginning in 1954, for national telecasts of all its championship games. Most of the television stations in North Carolina carried UNC's triple-overtime semifinal win over Michigan State and its triple-overtime championship victory over Kansas in the 1957 Final Four.

So successful was the NCAA venture in '57 that Chesley began his regular ACC telecasts in the 1957-58 season. The first game was UNC-Clemson on Dec. 7, 1957, and Chesley's network carried 11 games on successive Saturdays that season. Pilot Life Insurance was the sponsor; Jim Simpson and Bill Creasy were the announcers.

ACC basketball — often featuring the Tar Heels — has been a television staple ever since.

Tommy Kearns was a benefit of McGuire's New York connections.

ejected for a flagrant foul, Gotkin was assessed a technical, and when free throws were exchanged, State led 52-51. Pack star Ron Shavlik missed a free throw with four seconds left, but Herb Applebaum rebounded to preserve the State victory.

Rosenbluth, Young and Hilliard Greene joined the club for the 1954-55 season, and Rosenbluth was as good as advertised, averaging 25.5 points and 11.7 rebounds to become UNC's first All-ACC first-team selection. The Heels beat State again, 84-80, at Reynolds on Jan. 18, with the starting five — Rosenbluth, Vayda, Young, Radovich and Lifson — playing the whole game. Rosenbluth scored 22 and Vayda 19. Carolina riddled the Wolfpack's zone defense, shooting 54.6 percent in the first half.

The Tar Heels, however, slumped badly at the season's end, losing five of their last six regular-season games and again losing in the first round of the ACC Tournament to finish 10-11. Rosenbluth scored 29 points in his tournament debut, but Wake Forest's Dickie Hemric (33 points) and Lowell Davis (32) combined for 65 points in the Demon Deacons' 95-82 victory.

Help was on the way, though. McGuire's New York connections had produced a freshman class that included Tommy Kearns, Pete Brennan and Bob Cunningham, plus Joe Quigg, who'd sat out a year for academics. Those four, plus Rosenbluth, would produce a national championship two years later.

PRELUDE TO A TITLE At the beginning of the season, all the pieces were in place. Kearns, Brennan, Cunningham and Quigg, plus Ken Rosemond, joined Rosenbluth, Vayda, Young, McCabe and Greene, giving McGuire the depth the Tar Heels had lacked in previous seasons.

At times, the combination was awesome. The Heels scored a school-record 101 points in a rout of Virginia on Jan. 10, 1956, and 103 points in two overtimes against Clemson on Jan. 14, when Rosenbluth scored 45 to tie George Glamack's single-game scoring record. Rosenbluth scored 45 again, and Vayda added 25, in a 115-63 mauling of William & Mary on Feb. 7.

The Tar Heels beat State again, 73-69 on Jan. 18, avenging an earlier loss to the Wolfpack in the Dixie Classic finals. Brennan scored 20 points and snapped a 67-67 tie with a free throw with two minutes left. Rosenbluth registered 23, including the last four points to ice the win.

Carolina tied with State for the ACC regular-season title, but again, Wake Forest was waiting in the tournament. Rosenbluth scored 35 in a first-round win over Virginia and 26 against Wake. However, the Tar

TAR HEELS QUIZ

6. What early Carolina coach later became a renowned surgeon?

Heels hit only 19 of 75 shots and lost to the Deacons 77-56 to finish the season with an 18-5 record. Carolina would not lose again to the Deacons or anybody else for more than a year.

1956-57: NATIONAL CHAMPS

TAR HEELS QUIZ

Frank McGuire expected to have a good team in 1956-57, but he did not expect his Tar Heels to challenge for the national championship. That, McGuire figured, was another year, maybe two, away.

"There was something eerie about winning 32 straight," McGuire said. "We won several games we should have lost. We got breaks that were out of this world. I thought for sure we would lose at least four games we won.

"Finally, I almost hoped we could get beaten just to take the terrific pressure off the players."

By January 1957, Chapel Hill was one tingling, quaking bundle of nerves. Fans were inundating the basketball office with rabbit's feet and four-leafed clovers. One professor refused to change his suit for a month for fear he'd jinx the team. One student collected several months' worth of parking tickets, afraid that if he moved his car, the Tar Heels might lose.

Everyone was on edge — except the players.

Their nerves had been settled before the season began. McGuire had made it clear that Lennie Rosenbluth was to be the star, a plan that did not sit well with some others in the lineup. Rather than iron it out himself, McGuire told Rosenbluth that it was his job, as captain, to settle matters.

A day later, Rosenbluth told the coach, "We had a meeting and settled it. Some of it was my fault, and some was theirs. There's nothing to worry about from now on."

A week later, on Dec. 3, the Tar Heels opened the season against Furman. Rosenbluth scored 47 points, a school record, and Carolina won, 94-66.

ON A ROLL The first big test came at South Carolina on Dec. 15. The Tar Heels trailed by three with 40 seconds left. Rosenbluth missed a shot, but Stan Groll, a reserve, grabbed the rebound and kicked the ball out to Tommy Kearns. Kearns drove to the basket, made the layup, was fouled and sank the free throw to tie the game. UNC pulled away to win 90-86.

By Dec. 20, Carolina was 5-0 and ranked No. 3 in the nation. In Madison Square Garden, NYU blanketed Rosenbluth and held the Tar Heel star to nine points. However, Pete Brennan scored 16 and Joe Quigg 14, and the Heels led all the way in a 64-59 win.

7. When was the first formal basketball "game" played on the Carolina campus?

The NCAA field was expanded from eight teams to 16 in 1951, with 10 conferences, including the Southern, receiving automatic bids. The number of regional sites was increased from two to four in 1952. In 1953, the field was expanded to 22 teams. The number fluctuated from 22 to 25 until a 32-team bracket was adopted in 1975.

Guard Tommy Kearns (40), here in action against Wake Forest, was Carolina's top ball-handler from 1955 to 1958 and a major contributor to the Tar Heels' 1957 title.

Utah was unbeaten going into its first-round game against the Tar Heels in the Dixie Classic, and coach Jack Gardner predicted the Heels weren't quick enough to stay with his team's withering fast break. Before Gardner could take his seat on the Reynolds Coliseum bench, Carolina was ahead 22-4 en route to a 97-76 victory.

The closest calls came later, against Maryland and Duke.

On Feb. 5 at College Park, Rosenbluth fouled out after scoring 25, and the Terrapins led 53-49 with less than two minutes to go. Kearns and Bob Cunningham rallied the Heels to a 53-53 tie, and then Quigg blocked a shot at the buzzer to send the game into overtime. The Terps missed at the overtime horn, leaving the score 59-59 and forcing a second extra period. Kearns broke the deadlock with 1:50 to go in the second OT, and Carolina held on to win, 65-61.

Four days later at Duke, it seemed only Rosenbluth could find the basket, and the senior captain scored 35 points to keep the Tar Heels in front. Then, the Blue Devils rallied, erasing a 73-65 deficit to tie the score at 73 with 16 seconds left. Kearns was fouled, went to the line and coolly dropped through both free throws for a 75-73 win.

DANGEROUS DEACS Wake Forest's team that season featured four superb seniors in Jack Murdoch, Ernie Wiggins, Jack Williams and Jim Gilley. The Demon Deacons, coached by Murray Greason and with Bones

McKinney as assistant coach, finished 19-9.

Four of Wake's nine losses were to Carolina, and each game was a classic.

The two teams first met on Dec. 29 in the Dixie Classic finals in Raleigh. The game was the most lopsided of the four, with UNC jumping to a 19-2 lead and coasting to its first Classic title, 63-55.

The matchup in Chapel Hill on Feb. 13 was much closer. Carolina again led most of the way, before Wake Forest staged a furious comeback and pulled to within a point with a minute to go. The diminutive Kearns, however, knocked in two free throws with 16 seconds left and another one with one second to go to ice a 72-69 win.

The pressure mounted as the season progressed. On Feb. 26, the Tar Heels were 22-0, but the gutsy homestanding Deacons led by as many as eight points in the second half and had Carolina on the ropes 63-62 with 46 seconds left. Then Cunningham stole a Wake pass and scored to put the Heels in front. Seconds later, Brennan was fouled and went to the foul line. He missed his first one.

McKinney stood up at the Wake bench and yelled across the floor, "Don't choke, Brennan!"

Brennan laughed, then nailed his second shot for a 66-63 Tar Heel lead. And as he ran downcourt, Brennan passed the Deacons' bench. "How's that for choking, Bones?" he asked.

The two teams traded free throws, then Kearns

Pete Brennan helped the Tar Heels defeat Wake Forest four times during the 1956-57 season — in the Dixie Classic final, twice during the regular season and again in the ACC Tournament.

The Tar Heels, led by Rosenbluth (holding the net), celebrate the 63-55 victory over Wake Forest that gave Carolina the Dixie Classic title in December 1956.

TAR HEELS QUIZ

8. What former Tar
Heel player and
coach won 12
varsity letters in his
playing career at
UNC?

converted a three-point play with five seconds left. After his final foul toss, Kearns ran across the court and jumped into Bob Young's arms as the Tar Heels celebrated their 69-64 victory.

The last meeting, in the ACC Tournament, was the most critical. Carolina had crushed Clemson 81-61 in the first round, with Rosenbluth scoring 45 points, an ACC Tournament record that still stands.

A loss to the Deacons would have sent the Tar Heels home to Chapel Hill with nothing to show for their 25-game winning streak. Wake Forest had handled N.C. State easily, 66-56, in its tournament opener.

As in the three earlier meetings, Carolina took the early lead. And again, the Deacons staged a furious rally, erasing a 58-53 deficit in the last 2:30 to go ahead 59-58 with 46 seconds remaining.

Rosenbluth, who finished with 23 points, tossed in a hook shot, was fouled and canned the free throw for the 61-59 victory.

The ACC final against South Carolina was an anticlimax. Rosenbluth scored 38 points — a record for the ACC championship game until Charlie Scott broke it with 40 in 1967 — and the Tar Heels crushed the Gamecocks, 95-75. UNC had won its first ACC Tournament title and the Tar Heels' first postseason championship since 1945.

NCAA EAST Since the Tar Heels' last NCAA appearance in 1946, the field had been expanded from eight to 22-25 teams and sites added to include four regionals. Carrying a gaudy 27-0 record and a No. 1 national ranking, the Heels were bracketed to play Yale in a first-round game in Madison Square Garden on March 12.

The Elis proved a bit tougher than expected. Rosenbluth scored 16 points before picking up his fourth foul and going to the bench with 16 minutes left and Yale ahead, 62-60. Even with their senior captain on the sidelines, the Tar Heels surged. Kearns and Cunningham led the rally, then Quigg scored six straight points to help UNC forge in front 76-65 before going on to win, 90-74.

Rosenbluth finished with 29 points, Brennan had 20, Kearns 16, Quigg 13, and Cunningham 12.

It was on to Philadelphia, and McGuire was nervous. "I'm taking (nerve) pills for the first time in my life," the coach said on the eve of the Tar Heels' regional semifinal against Canisius. "The boys are OK, but I'm not."

McGuire shouldn't have worried. Rosenbluth scored 23 in the first half and finished with 39. The Heels led 39-25 at halftime and won easily, 87-75.

The East Regional final also was a breeze. Carolina jumped to a nine-point lead against Syracuse and stayed

Joe Quigg earned second-team All-ACC Tournament honors in 1957. His two free throws in the third overtime gave UNC a 54-53 victory against Kansas in the '57 championship game.

CAROLINA BLUE AND WHITE

Carolina's team colors — light blue and white — originated in the post-Civil War days.

When the university reopened after the war, students were required to join one of the campus' two literary societies. The Dialectic Society was composed primarily of students from the western half of the state; the Philanthropic Society was made up mostly of students from the east.

University honors — such as marshals, spring dance leaders, etc. — usually were awarded to an equal number of students from each society, and on such special occasions, the students wore the official color of their society, light blue for the Dialectic, white for the Philanthropic. The chief honorary, like the chief marshal, wore both colors, to represent the entire body of students.

When intercollegiate athletics became popular, the university had no officials colors, so students and fans naturally adopted the two colors — light blue and white — as representative of the entire student body.

Today, the primary color is registered as PMS #297. It goes by many names — light blue, powder blue, sky blue, Columbia blue — but to Tar Heels, it's just Carolina Blue.

---

in front, winning 67-58. Rosenbluth netted 25, Kearns had 22, and Brennan chipped in 13.

Next stop — Kansas City.

SPARTAN EFFORT *News & Observer* sports editor Dick Herbert called Carolina's triple-overtime, 74-70 victory over Michigan State in the national semifinals "one of the all-time great NCAA playoff games."

He didn't know, of course, that it was just a warm-up for the championship.

The Spartans and their 6-foot-5 sophomore star Johnny Green extended UNC to the limit, threatening to end the Tar Heels' run one game short of the national title. As they had all season, the Heels fought back, coolly and confidently, and with a multitude of heroes.

The high-leaping Green dogged Rosenbluth throughout the night, and neither team ever enjoyed a comfortable lead. Cunningham's three-point play at the buzzer earned the Tar Heels a 29-29 tie at halftime.

The second half produced more of the same. Green tied the score at 58-58 with two free throws with 1:57 left, and UNC held the ball for a final shot. Kearns' 20-footer bounded off the rim, and the Spartans' Jack Quiggle grabbed the rebound, raced to midcourt and flung up a 50-foot shot that hit the backboard and banked in. Many in the wildly cheering crowd of 10,000 didn't realize the shot didn't count until the teams

TAR HEELS QUIZ

9. Who coached UNC's first national championship team?

returned to the floor to begin the first overtime period.

At the end of the first overtime, the Tar Heels again were teetering on the edge of elimination. Michigan State led 64-62 with Green at the foul line with 11 seconds to go. Green missed. Brennan snatched the rebound, whirled and sprinted downcourt. With two seconds showing, he pulled up at 10 feet and fired in a jumper for a 64-64 tie and a second overtime.

Two tired teams managed a basket apiece in the second overtime. Cunningham and Quigg went to the UNC bench with five fouls during the period, and Brennan soon followed. Reserves Young, Danny Lotz and Roy Searcy came on to fill in admirably, and Rosenbluth missed a 20-footer at the buzzer, leading to the third overtime.

In the third overtime, Rosenbluth, who finished with 31 points, took charge. He scored two quick baskets, finally giving the Heels some breathing room, and then took over most of the ball handling. Kearns hit two clutch free throws, and Young followed a Rosenbluth miss to give Carolina a 74-68 lead with 1:30 to play. Searcy helped protect the lead with two crucial rebounds in the last minute.

The 74-70 victory set off a frenzied celebration in Chapel Hill. More than 1,000 students gathered on Franklin Street, stopped traffic, sang "Hark The Sound," threw toilet paper and cheered. There was no vandalism, and police reported no arrests.

Once again, Carolina would play for the national championship. And once again, a giant stood between the Tar Heels and the title.

TAR HEELS QUIZ

10. Who built the first basketball court at UNC?

GIANT KILLERS Bob Kurland, Oklahoma A&M's 7-foot giant in the '46 finals, had been nicknamed "the mechanical man." That description did not fit Wilt Chamberlain, Kansas' 7-foot-2 sophomore.

"The Big Dipper" — Chamberlain preferred that to the more-often heard "Wilt the Stilt" — had averaged 29.6 points and 18.9 rebounds that season. He had scored 32 points and grabbed 18 rebounds in the semifinals, when the Jayhawks demolished defending national champion San Francisco, 80-56.

"Our entire approach had to be geared to one man, Wilt Chamberlain," McGuire said. "In the dressing room before the game, I told the boys only a few basic things.

"I said I didn't care if we didn't take a single shot in the first half if the shot opportunity wasn't a good one … Our job was to box him out from under the boards."

If McGuire was an expert when it came to X's and O's, he was a genius when it came to psychology. When Chamberlain stepped into the circle for the opening tip-off, he looked down on the head of the 5-foot-10 Kearns.

"I can still see Chamberlain's face as Kearns lined up to jump against him," McGuire recalled in *Tar Heel.* "Wilt looked 10 feet tall towering over Tommy, but they made such a ridiculous picture together that Chamberlain must have felt no bigger than his thumb. At least, that's the state of mind we wanted to get him into.

"North Carolina had to stop Chamberlain to win, and anything we could do to harass him would help. We wanted him thinking, 'Is this coach crazy? What other tricks does he have up his sleeve?' What I wanted was for Chamberlain to get a good shock."

It worked. Chamberlain controlled the tip, but he missed his first shot and didn't score until five minutes into the game. By that time, Carolina was ahead 9-2.

SHOT SELECTION Kansas opened in a box-and-one defense, with Rosenbluth getting the extra coverage. McGuire had hoped the Jayhawks would follow this strategy.

The Tar Heels spread the floor, held the ball and waited patiently for an opening. When the opening came, the Heels struck quickly.

When the ball did go up, on either end of the floor, the Tar Heels' first objective was to keep Chamberlain away from the basket. Joe Quigg played in front of the big man, and when the ball went up, the next-closest player was to join Quigg to form a two-man screen

Lennie Rosenbluth rebounds against Wake Forest in one of the UNC-Deacon thrillers in 1956-57.

between Chamberlain and the basket. The next-closest Tar Heel went for the rebound.

In the first half, Rosenbluth hit five of his seven shots, going to the locker room with 14 points. The Heels shot a remarkable 64.7 percent from the field and out-rebounded the Jayhawks 17-10. Chamberlain had two field goals and eight points, and Carolina led 29-22 at the break.

JAYHAWKS RALLY North Carolina couldn't maintain that pace, and a 10-point Jayhawk surge early in the second half gave Kansas the lead.

Then, the Jayhawks made a critical error. With a three-point lead and about seven minutes remaining, Kansas held the ball.

At that point, the Tar Heels were reeling. They were dog-tired, having played a triple overtime game the night before against Michigan State. And they were in foul trouble — Rosenbluth and Kearns had three apiece and Quigg had been called for four.

The Kansas City crowd loved it, figuring the Jayhawks were giving the Heels a taste of their own medicine. McGuire loved it, too, knowing the Kansas stall was giving his team a chance to catch its breath. With five minutes to go, McGuire raised his hand, a signal for the Tar Heels to pick up the pace again. Kansas had lost its advantage.

Dick Harp's Kansas team went three overtimes before falling to Carolina in 1957. Three decades later, Harp was on the Carolina bench as an assistant to Dean Smith.

OVERTIME TIMES 3 (AGAIN) Still, with 1:45 to go, Carolina was in deep trouble. Rosenbluth had fouled out with the Jayhawks holding a 46-43 lead.

It wasn't over yet, though. Quigg hit a short jumper to bring UNC to within one. Then Bob Cunningham rebounded a Kansas miss, and Kearns tied the score 46-46 with a free throw. Cunningham missed a last-second shot, sending the game into overtime.

The teams traded baskets in the first overtime, and tempers flared when Brennan and Chamberlain collided under the Kansas basket. McGuire protested vehemently, and Kansas coach Dick Harp, later to be a UNC assistant coach under Dean Smith, told McGuire to shut up. Later, the two head coaches shook hands.

Carolina controlled the ball in the closing seconds, but Kearns' driving shot at the buzzer was batted away by Chamberlain.

Neither team scored in the second OT, although Kansas had the game-winning opportunity. With 10 seconds remaining, a jump ball was called when a dribbling Brennan was closely guarded by Jayhawk sophomore Ron Loneski. Kansas won the tip, and Loneski got an open shot from the corner but missed.

QUIGG, THE HERO Finally, in the third overtime, Carolina seemed to have the situation in hand. Kearns scored on a driving shot, then added two free throws, and the Tar Heels led 52-48 with 3:47 to go.

Kansas made one last, valiant charge. Chamberlain scored, was fouled by Cunningham and made his free throw, quickly slicing UNC's lead to a point at 52-51.

With 2:33 left, the Jayhawks made the first of two free throws to pull even at 52-52. Then, after Kansas stole the ball from Quigg, Kearns was whistled for a deliberate foul.

With 31 seconds remaining, the Jayhawks missed the first foul shot but made the second to go ahead 53-52.

McGuire called timeout to set up a final play.

With about 10 seconds to go, Quigg made his move, driving toward the basket. He was fouled immediately.

McGuire called timeout again. In the Tar Heels' huddle, assistant coach Buck Freeman told Quigg, "Don't

There's some disagreement over who threw the lob pass to Wilt Chamberlain that was tipped away by Joe Quigg at the end of the 1957 championship game. Some UNC sources say it was Gene Elstun; Kansas sources and some UNC sources say Ron Loneski.

Joe Quigg hit the game-winning free throws with six seconds left in the third overtime against Kansas, but just as important was Quigg's defensive work on Jayhawks star Wilt Chamberlain.

forget to follow through and end up on your toes."

The pressure was unbearable as the teams filed back onto the floor and Quigg stepped to the foul line. His first two-handed push shot went up and in to tie the game at 53.

His second shot was the same, and the Tar Heels led 54-53.

"I had just missed an important free throw before, and I was nervous then," Quigg said later. "This time I was not nervous at all. I concentrated on rising to my toes, as the coach told me I should."

Kansas had one last gasp, with five seconds to go, and Quigg, again, was the hero.

The Jayhawks quickly moved the ball downcourt, and lobbed the ball high to Chamberlain in the middle, trying to set up "The Big Dipper" for his unstoppable dunk shot. But Quigg, who had fronted Chamberlain all night, leaped high to knock the ball away with one hand.

Quigg's tip went straight into the hands of Kearns. The littlest Tar Heel dribbled twice, then slung the ball two-handed high into the rafters. When it landed, Carolina was the national champion.

THE STATS Although Carolina's shooting cooled considerably in the second half, the Heels still shot 46.7 percent for the game. They took just 45 shots.

Rosenbluth scored 20 points, hitting eight of 15 attempts, before fouling out. Kearns and Brennan had 11 points apiece, and Quigg scored 10.

The Tar Heels used only seven players. Kearns, Brennan and Cunningham each played the full 55

The 1957 NCAA Champion Tar Heels, (first row, left to right) manager Joel Fleischman, Stan Groll, Danny Lotz, Pete Brennan, Bob Cunningham, Tony Radovich, Harvey Salz, (back row) Coach Frank McGuire, Tommy Kearns, Ken Rosemond, Roy Searcy, Bill Hathaway, Joe Quigg, Lennie Rosenbluth, Gehrmann Holland, trainer John Lacey and assistant coach Buck Freeman.

minutes. Lotz replaced Rosenbluth, and Young subbed briefly for Quigg.

McGuire's plan to keep Chamberlain off the boards was astoundingly effective. The big man collected half of Kansas' rebounds, while the Tar Heels won the battle of the boards 42-28.

Chamberlain scored 23 points, seven below his season average.

CELEBRATION TIME As expected, the national championship victory set off another celebration in Chapel Hill.

About 3,000 students gathered on Franklin Street, set a bonfire, paraded, cheered and sang until well past midnight. Several carloads of students set off for Duke,

THE RAM

The idea for North Carolina's mascot — the ram — came about in 1924.

Victor Huggins, UNC's head cheerleader at the time, noticed many of the South's college football teams had an animal mascot and thought Carolina's team needed one, too. The star of the Tar Heels' team at that time was Jack Merritt, a big, bruising fullback whose nickname was "the Battering Ram," so Huggins settled on a ram.

Charles Woollen, the school's athletic business manager, liked the idea and gave Huggins $25 to purchase a ram. Huggins found a suitable ram in Texas and had it shipped to Chapel Hill in early November 1924.

The ram, dubbed Rameses I, arrived just in time for the Tar Heels' football game against Virginia Military on Nov. 8. It was a hard-fought contest, and with the teams locked in a scoreless tie late in the game, Bunn Hackney — who also was a basketball player and the Tar Heels' basketball captain in 1926-27 — was called on to attempt a field goal.

Heading onto the field, Hackney stopped and rubbed the ram's head for luck. He then drop-kicked a 30-yard field goal to give UNC a 3-0 victory.

Rameses has been a fixture at Tar Heel football games ever since. A new ram, Rameses XXVII, took the field in 1996.

The ram has not been a fixture at basketball games, however. In fact, Rameses I made the mascot's first and only indoor appearance at a game in the Indoor Athletic Court (the Tin Can) in 1924. Once in the gym, the ram did what farm animals are prone to do — on the floor — and was quickly banished.

Since the late 1960s, a student dressed in a ram costume has served as Rameses' stand-in for basketball.

TAR HEELS QUIZ

11. What was the official name of the "Tin Can"?

made the rounds near Duke Chapel, delivered the joyous news to their archrivals and departed. There were no reports of violence or damage on either campus.

The following day, a crowd estimated at more than 10,000 — students, fans and curious on-lookers — met the national champs at Raleigh-Durham Airport. So overwhelming was the throng that it broke through airport security barriers and spilled onto the runway before airport personnel moved the crowd back to allow the Tar Heels' plane to land.

Once off the plane, the players were mobbed. They were lifted onto the shoulders of the crowd and paraded around the runway.

Governor Luther Hodges, himself a former Tar Heel player, had been in Kansas City for the championship, and his plane landed about 30 minutes after the Tar Heels' plane. He and other state and university officials tried to conduct an official "welcome home" for the new champions, but the ceremonies essentially were canceled when the speakers couldn't be heard above the cheers of the crowd.

The players were carried away — literally and figuratively — by the reception. "Really, it's just too much," Brennan said. "Just too much."

When the airport celebration finally subsided, the team was whisked back to Chapel Hill, where more than a thousand students awaited for an "official" reception in Woollen Gym.

Two important members of the team missed it all. McGuire stayed in Kansas City, where he was to coach in the East-West All-Star Game that night. Rosenbluth flew from Kansas City to New York, where he was to appear that night on a national television show to accept the award as the Helms Foundation National Player of the Year.

TROUBLE IN PARADISE The seeds of McGuire's undoing at Carolina were sewn with the national championship in 1957.

Following the 32-0 season, it seemed everyone jumped on the Tar Heel bandwagon. McGuire expected his unprecedented success to open doors and, more importantly, to open the pocketbooks of the University's Board of Trustees and the state legislature. The coach lobbied for a new, larger arena, one befitting the national champion. Certainly, a larger coliseum was needed. The Tar Heels had to share Woollen Gym with physical education classes, and for games, seating was adequate for less than half the still-growing student body. He also wanted more money for recruiting and more freedom to operate his program as he saw fit.

Jim Tatum's return to Chapel Hill in 1956 precipitated a power struggle between Tatum's football program and McGuire's basketball team, but the two coaches remained friends.

None of that was forthcoming. In fact, the budget got tighter when Jim Tatum was lured back to Chapel Hill in 1956 to rebuild UNC's football program. Tatum was a Tar Heel star in the 1930s and coached the UNC football team during World War II. He left Chapel Hill for Maryland after the war and won a national championship with the Terrapins in 1953.

Both McGuire and Tatum were ambitious, strong-willed men. They fought hard for their programs — against the administration and against each other.

By 1959, when Tatum died suddenly from Rocky Mountain spotted fever, some of the luster of the '57 championship had faded. McGuire's battles with the administration continued and, in fact, became even more bitter.

FALL FROM GRACE It didn't help that McGuire's 1957-58 unit was a shadow of the national championship team.

Rosenbluth had graduated; he played briefly as a professional before beginning a long and successful career as a high school teacher and coach in Florida. Gone, too, were Young and Radovich, who had played the first half of the '57 season.

An injury sidelined Quigg for the season, further depleting the Tar Heels.

Carolina's winning streak ended early, six games into the season. West Virginia, led by Jerry West, beat the Heels, 75-64, in the final of the Kentucky Invitational at Lexington on Dec. 21, ending the streak at 37 games.

The Tar Heels lost five more games, and then were upset by Maryland in the ACC Tournament championship to finish 19-7.

Brennan led the team, averaging 21.3 points, and was a consensus All-American. He completed his career with 1,332 points, then second on UNC's all-time list behind Rosenbluth's 2,045.

L&M BOYS In '59, Carolina rebounded, thanks to another influx of New York talent. McGuire's sophomore class that year included York Larese, Doug Moe and Lou Brown and a Virginian, 6-foot-8 Dick Kepley. Lee Shaffer, a Pittsburgh native who had averaged 11 points the year before, was back as a junior.

Larese and Moe had been major catches for McGuire's N.Y. connection, "Uncle Harry" Gotkin.

Larese, a sweet-shooting 6-foot-4 wingman, was ticketed for N.C. State, but Gotkin got his foot in the door. Larese reneged on an early commitment to State and its talent scout, Howie Garfinkel, and signed on at UNC.

Moe wasn't as physically talented as Larese, but was a

Pete Brennan was the star of McGuire's post-championship team in '58, earning first-team All-America honors and being named ACC Player of the Year.

Carolina's first set of L&M Twins, Doug Moe (left) and York Larese, earned All-America recognition in 1959, '60 and '61.

Lee Shaffer averaged 18.2 points and 11.2 rebounds and was ACC Player of the Year as a senior in 1960. He also was the father of Lee Shaffer Jr., a star linebacker on UNC football teams in 1979-81.

tenacious defensive player, an excellent rebounder (though only 6-foot-5) and had an incredible instinct for the game.

Larese, averaging 15.1 points, Shaffer and Moe led the Heels to a 20-5 record and the ACC regular-season title that season. Carolina was ranked No. 1 in the nation after beating State on Jan. 14 and held that spot until back-to-back losses at Maryland and Virginia in late February.

The Heels lost to N.C. State, 80-56, in the ACC Tournament championship, but moved on to the NCAA playoffs, replacing the Wolfpack which had been barred from postseason play because of recruiting violations. The NCAA appearance, which was to be McGuire's last with the Tar Heels, ended quickly, with a 76-63 loss to Navy in Madison Square Garden.

MODERATE SUCCESS The presence of Shaffer, Larese, Moe and later Donnie Walsh, Larry Brown and Jim Hudock assured the Tar Heels of some success over the next two seasons.

In 1960, Carolina went 18-6 and shared the ACC regular-season crown with Wake Forest, although Moe missed the first half of the season on academic suspension for cutting too many classes. Shaffer, then a senior, led the ACC in scoring (18.2) and made the basketball writers' All-America team. However, Duke knocked the Heels out of the ACC Tournament in the semifinals, 71-69.

In 1961, Larese averaged 23.1 points, and Moe 20.4 points and 14 rebounds. Both earned All-America mention, while the Tar Heels won the ACC regular-season outright, finishing 19-4.

FIGHTIN' TAR HEELS McGuire's frustrations were starting to spill over onto the court, however. The coach's "us-against-the-world" attitude didn't engender much sympathy away from the cozy confines of Woollen Gym.

Against N.C. State in the '58 season, McGuire pulled his team off the court when the Reynolds Coliseum crowd lustily booed the Tar Heel players during pregame introductions. Everett Case later apologized for the crowd's behavior.

At Wake Forest in 1959, Shaffer tangled with a Wake player on a rebound, the Deacons' Dave Budd intervened, and a bench-clearing brawl ensued, involving a handful of Wake fans.

Larry Brown was a backcourt star for UNC in the early 1960s and now coaches in the NBA.

"The fracas finally ended," Dick Herbert wrote in *The News & Observer*, "after about 40 people were on the court — half fighting and the others trying to stop it."

McGuire and Deacons' coach Bones McKinney were censured by ACC Commissioner Jim Weaver for "failing to control their benches," and the league ordered the 1960 meeting between the schools be moved from Winston-Salem to a neutral site in Greensboro.

The capper came on Feb. 4, 1961, at Duke. The Tar Babies and the Blue Devil freshmen set the stage with a bench-clearing brawl in the preliminary game. The varsity game was uneventful until nine seconds remained, when, with Duke leading 80-75, Blue Devils' star Art Heyman and Larry Brown tangled while scrambling for a rebound. Fisticuffs ensued, with players from both teams and several Duke students getting involved before police broke the melee up.

Donnie Walsh was banned after the 1961 fight with Duke. Also banned for the season were Larry Brown and Duke's Art Heyman.

Referee Charlie Eckman ejected Heyman, claiming the Blue Devil had swung first, and awarded Brown two free throws. Duke eventually won, 81-77.

Three days later, Eckman told reporters that he'd looked at a film of the game and decided he was wrong. Brown had fouled Heyman, the ref said, and then several Carolina players had attacked Heyman.

Almost two weeks were needed to sort the situation out — although the whole incident had lasted only a matter of seconds. On Feb. 15, commissioner Weaver

Big Jim Hudock, Larry Brown and Donnie Walsh were stalwarts for McGuire's "fightin' Tar Heels" team in 1961. All three stayed on to help ease the transition for new coach Dean Smith.

ruled that Heyman, Brown and UNC's Donnie Walsh, who had joined in the fight, were banned for the rest of the season. The ACC's executive committee upheld the ruling the next day, and UNC Chancellor Aycock chose not to appeal.

McGuire blamed the whole incident on Duke.

"This has been blown out of proportion," he said. "This was all arranged by (Duke AD) Eddie Cameron. I know how they operate over there."

Lou Brown and Peppy Callahan were added to the varsity roster to replace Larry Brown and Walsh.

BEGINNING OF THE END McGuire was angered by the ACC ruling and stung by what he perceived as the UNC administration's lack of support. All that added to the coach's disenchantment with the situation at UNC.

But then, 1960-61 had not been the best of seasons for McGuire.

On Jan. 10, the NCAA had placed Carolina on one-year probation for irregularities in recruiting. The charges stemmed from mid-1958 and included "excessive entertainment of basketball players, prospective players and their parents."

The NCAA also censured the university and McGuire for "inadequate and ineffective accounting procedures." Some of the payments in question involved reimbursements for Harry Gotkin's expenses (legal at the time).

NCAA executive director Walter Byers said the charges against Carolina originated "outside of the Atlantic Coast Conference area," and a national magazine reported, although it was never substantiated, the NCAA had been tipped off by Howie Garfinkel.

The probation kept the Tar Heels out of invitational

Reimbursement for expenses to "talent scouts" like Harry Gotkin was legal until NCAA rules changes outlawed such recruiting in the early 1970s. NCAA charges against UNC centered on poor accounting practices and lack of documentation for these payments, not on illegal payments.

and postseason play in 1961, although UNC was allowed to participate in the Dixie Classic during the probationary period. With no opportunity to advance to the NCAA playoffs, Aycock withdrew the Heels from the 1961 ACC Tournament.

If that wasn't enough, just before the season began, the university declared 6-foot-7 Ken McComb, one of McGuire's top reserves, ineligible for academic reasons. A few weeks later, the ACC placed Billy Galantai, a freshman and another of McGuire's New Yorkers, on probation for misrepresenting a fact on his eligibility statement. Galantai eventually played as a reserve on the '63 and '64 teams.

McGuire's troubles were only beginning. On March

Jim Hudock (33) hit 50 percent of his shots to lead the Heels from the field in 1961. He earned second-team All-ACC honors that season.

17, 1961, the New York District Attorney's Office announced that two New York men, Aaron Wagman and Joseph Hacken, had been charged in a widespread conspiracy to "fix" college basketball games.

THE 'FIX' Within a month, the New York investigation had expanded to include players at more than 20 schools. Among them was North Carolina.

On April 27, indictments handed down in New York named Tar Heels senior Lou Brown as a co-conspirator, charging that Brown had worked with Jerry Vogel, a former Alabama player, and Wagman in an attempt to shave points in games stretching back to the 1958 season.

In addition, the investigations revealed that Brown had attempted to induce Carolina teammates Moe and Ray Stanley to shave points and that Moe had taken a $75 payoff, although he never intended to act on the plan. Stanley, an outstanding student and a member of the University's Order of the Golden Fleece, one of its highest honorary societies, turned the offer down flat, but like Moe, did not report the bribe attempt to authorities.

The scandal eventually would touch 22 schools and 39 players.

THE FIXER Lou Brown had been one of "Uncle Harry" Gotkin's boys, a poor kid from the tough Jersey City, N.J., streets. He'd been a star at St. Michael's High — the first player in that school's history to score 1,000 points — and had been highly recruited. Duke, N.C. State and Kentucky, as well as UNC, were among his suitors.

Brown was the leading scorer on Carolina's freshman team in 1958, but once on the varsity, he got little playing time. Discouraged, unhappy and short of money, Brown was ripe for the picking, and "The Bagman" found him.

Aaron "The Bagman" Wagman met Brown on Dec. 4, 1959. The year before, Brown had been approached by Vogel, whom he'd met several summers earlier when the two had worked at a Catskills Mountains resort. Vogel outlined a plan to "fix" college games, and Brown said he refused. Then Vogel asked if he'd meet "a man," and Brown agreed.

From Brown's later testimony, Wagman, who had been convicted of attempting to bribe a Florida football player a year earlier, made it sound easy — $1,000 for the first game, $1,250 for the second, then more. Brown was hooked.

Wagman supplied the money, Brown made the contacts. The UNC senior helped Wagman connect with players at St. Joseph's, La Salle and Pitt.

He had less success with his own teammates. Stanley turned him down and Moe did, too. Wagman was

All-American Doug Moe admitted taking a $75 "gift" from gamblers, but otherwise was not implicated in the point-shaving scandals.

Lou Brown was termed "uncoopera- tive" by FBI and state investigators. Brown offered testimony to clear Doug Moe and Ray Stanley of game- fixing charges, but repeatedly denied his own involvement in the point-shaving schemes, although federal agents had filmed a number of his meetings with Aaron Wagman and Jerry Vogel.

insistent, and Brown eventually set up a meeting between Moe and "The Bagman" in September 1959.

At that meeting, Moe again refused to participate in the point-shaving scheme. Wagman gave him $75, as a "gift."

"I didn't see anything wrong in taking the money from Wagman for not doing anything," Moe explained later.

Brown met with Wagman a dozen times over the next year, to arrange fixes and to exchange payoff money. What neither knew was that New York State investigators and FBI agents were filming their meetings and gathering evidence.

THE FALLOUT When the scheme began to unravel in March 1961, it happened quickly.

Brown withdrew from the university on March 29, with the stipulation that he could not re-enroll without the permission of the chancellor. He was arrested and charged with conspiring to bribe players to fix games, was convicted and served time in prison.

Moe went before the university's Student Honor Council and was cleared of any wrongdoing. The following day, May 3, Chancellor Aycock suspended Moe indefinitely, not because he had taken money from the gamblers, but because he had lied to Aycock about his involvement. Moe, who had been scheduled to graduate in June, later returned to school and received his degree.

Stanley, who had graduated in 1960, was guilty only of failing to report a bribe attempt and was never charged.

The big blow came May 22. The Board of Trustees of the Consolidated University of North Carolina, following the lead of President William C. Friday, voted to de-emphasize basketball on all university campuses.

Friday's plan included the immediate abolition of the Dixie Classic, a reduced schedule (only two non-conference games outside the ACC and NCAA postseason tournaments), scholarship limitations (a limit of two scholarships per year for players from outside the ACC area) and a ban on organized summer competition.

McGUIRE'S EXIT Nobody, of course, laid blame for the scandals on McGuire. If anything, the UNC coach, who had a front-row seat in the point-shaving scandals of the early '50s, had been among the most vigilant.

"Every year at ACC meetings, Frank would implore coaches to keep their players mindful of the scandal of 1951," Bones McKinney said. "Many of the coaches, including myself, adopted programs similar to his in the matter of warning against bribe offers."

For McGuire, that made the situation even worse.

On May 4-5, 1961, several hundred students staged demonstrations on the UNC campus protesting Chancellor Aycock's suspension of Doug Moe. The protests centered on Aycock's failure to abide by the ruling of the Student Honor Council, which had found Moe not guilty. Aycock met with the students May 5, explained his reasons for the suspension, and the demonstrations ceased.

Charges were brought against some players, including Lou Brown, in both New York and North Carolina. North Carolina conducted its own investigations, funded by a $50,000 appropriation from the N.C. Legislature requested by Governor Terry Sanford.

In a speech in Charlotte on June 2, McGuire said he was determined to face the challenges now present at UNC.

"I can't quit. It's more of a challenge than ever," McGuire said. "I only want to do what I can — for the university, for basketball, for an end to these many problems."

Throughout the spring and summer of '61 reports circulated that McGuire would leave Carolina to take a job in the NBA. However, he turned down an offer to coach the New York Knickerbockers in June.

The Philadelphia Warriors also came calling, offering McGuire $15,000 a year, $3,000 more than he was making at UNC. He accepted the job once, changed his mind, and finally rejected a counter-offer.

Doug Moe, here rebounding against Maryland, was an all-around star for McGuire's last Tar Heel team.

Meanwhile at UNC, McGuire's troubles continued.

On June 10, Jim Donohue, a 6-8 junior reserve who had sat out the '61 season, was dismissed from the university for his part in stealing a gum ball machine from a Wilmington, N.C., hospital. Lou Brown also was charged in what Donohue said was "a stupid prank."

In late June, guard Billy Lawrence of New York, considered the top high school player in the country that year, reneged on his commitment to attend UNC, citing the cutbacks in the basketball program. Lawrence eventually attended St. John's.

Two days later, Judd Rathman, a highly recruited 6-foot-8 New Yorker, also pulled out of his agreement to enroll at Carolina.

McGuire felt an obligation to the players he did have coming in — including Billy Cunningham, who enrolled at UNC that summer — and to his assistant coaches. But the situation was becoming untenable.

In July, McGuire called Warriors' owner Eddie Gottlieb and asked to be considered again for the still-vacant coach's job.

On Aug. 1, 1961, Chancellor Aycock issued a statement:

"Head coach Frank McGuire has requested the University of North Carolina to release him in order that he may accept an offer to become head coach of the Philadelphia Warriors professional basketball team. … We are reluctant to lose him. We do not, however, wish to prevent his acceptance of this extremely attractive position. We have agreed to release him effective August 31, 1961, with regret, but with our deepest good wishes."

Two days later, in a news conference in Philadelphia, McGuire said he would not have left UNC had the Warriors not offered him a team vice-presidency in addition to the coaching job. It was an opportunity "within keeping with my long-range goals" he said.

"The situation at North Carolina had nothing to do with my decision to quit," McGuire added.

Nobody believed that.

12. Nat Cartmell, Carolina's first coach, was better known as a track and field performer. What was his specialty?

13. Which other school did Tar Heel All-American George Glamack attend before enrolling at UNC?

1961-78:
Making of a Legend

Dean Smith's Topeka High basketball team reached the state semifinals in his junior year, but was eliminated early in the state tournament in his senior season, losing to Wichita East, coached by Ralph Miller (later long-time head coach at Oregon State). In football, Smith quarterbacked Topeka to the state finals as a senior. His baseball team defeated Wichita North to win the state baseball championship in his senior year.

Frank McGuire had the last word at Carolina.

Thirty-year-old Dean Smith, a UNC assistant since 1958 and a virtual unknown outside the coaching community, was McGuire's choice as his successor. McGuire took his recommendation straight to Chancellor William Aycock, bypassing Athletic Director Chuck Erickson.

Erickson, it was rumored, favored Dan Nyimicz, who had captained the '49 UNC team under Tom Scott. But Erickson never had a chance.

McGuire knew it would be easy to sell Aycock on Smith. The chancellor had worked closely with Smith during the NCAA probation hearings and had been impressed with the young assistant. Still, Aycock asked McGuire if he would like to take a week to think over his recommendation. McGuire said no.

Dean Smith was introduced as Carolina's new head coach on Aug. 4, 1961.

DEAN WHO? If Smith wasn't well-known outside basketball circles, he was highly regarded within them.

Born in Emporia, Kan., the son of a teacher and a teacher-coach, Smith described his upbringing as "normal Middle American." He was an excellent student, excelling in math, and an outstanding athlete. The family moved to Topeka, Kan., after his freshman year in high school, and Smith was the quarterback in football, the point guard in basketball and the catcher in baseball, leading all three Topeka High teams to state finals.

He turned down a partial basketball scholarship to Kansas State to attend Kansas on an academic grant, partly because his father had gone there (for his master's degree) and partly because he greatly admired the Jayhawks'

Smith weighed only 155 pounds after his freshman year at Kansas. His father convinced him that his future was in basketball and baseball, not football.

coach, the legendary Phog Allen. Smith played football as a freshman at Kansas — giving it up on his father's advice — and lettered in baseball for three seasons.

But it was basketball that intrigued him, although he started only a couple of games and spent most of his college career on the Jayhawks' bench. He was the top backcourt reserve, averaging not quite two points a game, on Kansas teams that won the NCAA Championship in 1952 and finished as NCAA runner-up in '53.

"Looking back," Smith said modestly, "I was very mediocre at all three sports."

Mostly, Smith watched and listened, learning all he

could from Allen and his assistant, Dick Harp.

"It was obvious that the interest was there," said Harp, who later coached Kansas against the Tar Heels in the '57 NCAA Championship. "His dad had been a coach, and there was no question he was an analytical young man. … He was a bright person to begin with, was creative, and gave every evidence then of having the grasp on basketball which he has now."

Smith averaged 1.6 points as a junior on the Jayhawks' NCAA Championship team in 1951-52 and 2.1 points as a senior in 1952-53. He scored a total of 80 points in his college career.

Smith, like many KU athletes during the Korean War years, enrolled in the Air Force ROTC program and faced a two-year hitch upon graduation. While awaiting orders, he helped Harp coach the Kansas freshman team, and then after his assignment to Furstenfeldbruck, Germany, he played on and coached a military club.

"I'll always remember that team," Smith said. "We were undefeated, 11-0, while I was coaching. … All the members of that team really wanted to play, which made coaching easy, and it was great fun. That experience just whetted my appetite to coach."

THE ROAD TO CAROLINA While in Germany, Smith met Bob Spear, a former Navy assistant who was coaching an Air Force team in France. The two became close friends, and in 1956, when Spear was named head coach at the new Air Force Academy in Denver, he asked that Smith be made his assistant.

Bob Spear (left), here during a 1994 visit to Chapel Hill, was Smith's boss at the Air Force Academy and recommended his young assistant to North Carolina Coach Frank McGuire.

A few months were needed to make the arrangements, and Smith joined Spear in Denver in January 1956.

With Spear's experience and Smith's penchant for organization and innovation, Air Force went 11-10 in its first season and 17-6 in its second. Spear gave Smith

In the mid-1980s, Dick Harp came to Carolina and served two seasons as an administrative assistant on Smith's staff.

freedom to design and develop the offense and defense, and the Falcons used early versions of the run-and-jump and point-zone defenses that Carolina uses today. Smith also installed an early version of the Four Corners offense made famous by his Tar Heels in the 1970s.

Smith's stay at Air Force lasted two years. In 1957, Spear and Smith attended the national coaches' convention at the Final Four in Kansas City, where they shared a suite in the Continental Hotel with Spear's longtime friend, Ben Carnevale, and two of Carnevale's old friends — University of Denver coach Hoyt Brawner and Frank McGuire.

It was pretty impressive company for a 26-year-old with less than a year's experience as a college assistant coach, and Spear talked glowingly about his young aide.

At breakfast the morning after UNC's championship win over Kansas, McGuire broached the subject.

THE DEAN

It would take another book, twice the length of this one, to list all of the contributions that Dean Smith has made to college basketball.

From a technical standpoint, nearly every team in the country uses something — the run-and-jump defense, the free-lance passing game, multiple screens, the point zone, the scramble defense, etc. — that Smith either devised or perfected. His book, *Basketball: Multiple Offenses and Defenses*, is the best-selling technical book on basketball ever printed and has been read — and its tactics used — by coaches all over the world.

Even Smith's Carolina nuances — the foul-line huddle, multiple substitutions, acknowledging a good pass or play — have been copied by coaches and teams at every level.

His influence will be felt for many years to come. Thirty-nine of Smith's players have gone on to coach basketball, and eight — nine if you count Kansas' Roy Williams, who

did not play at UNC but was a Smith assistant coach — now hold head coaching jobs at the professional or major-college level.

UNC coach Dean Smith's contributions to college basketball are immeasurable.

As a teacher, Smith has few peers. In an interview in early 1996, Smith said he had had only three players in his coaching career — James Worthy, Sam Perkins and Rasheed Wallace — whom he felt, in their freshman seasons, were almost certain to become successful pro players. Yet, 48 Tar Heels who played under Smith have gone on to play professional basketball, earning all-league honors 41 times, receiving 20 season or postseason MVP awards and winning 20 league championships.

"That's when Frank said, 'Buck (Freeman) has been ill, and I may need an assistant next year or the following year. Bob and Ben tell me I should hire you,' " Smith recalled in *Dean Smith: A Biography.* "I said, 'I don't know; whatever Bob says.' "

Freeman stayed another year at UNC. However, at the coaches' convention in Louisville in 1958, McGuire told Smith that Freeman was retiring and invited him to Chapel Hill for a visit. By August, Smith was a Tar Heel, taking a pay cut in the process. He made less than $3,000 his first season.

McGuire had beaten others to the punch. A few months later, Brawner offered Smith an assistant's job at Denver, promising him the head coaching job the next year, when Brawner was to become athletic director. Smith actually got as far as the Raleigh-Durham Airport with a ticket to Denver in hand before changing his mind.

In addition to the Denver and Kansas job offers, Dean Smith also was offered the head coaching job at Wyoming in the early 1960s.

During his 35 seasons at UNC, the Tar Heels have won more games (851), earned more Top 10 rankings (23), appeared in more NCAA Tournaments (26) and won more NCAA Tournament games (61) than any school in the country. Under Smith, the Tar Heels have won or shared 18 ACC regular-season titles and won 12 ACC Tournament and 10 NCAA regional titles in addition to two NCAA championships and one National Invitation Tournament crown.

What is really remarkable about Smith's 35 seasons at North Carolina is the consistency.

His teams, competing in the toughest conference in the land, have won 20 or more games for 26 consecutive seasons. For 32 years, since 1964, the Tar Heels have finished no lower than third in the Atlantic Coast Conference regular season.

Since 1975, when the NCAA opened its tournament to allow more than one team from a conference, Carolina has advanced to postseason play in every season. It has won at least one game in every NCAA postseason tournament since 1980.

In Smith's 35 years, the Tar Heels have reached the NCAA's Sweet 16 on 20 occasions, have been in the Final Eight 14 times, the Final Four 10 times and played for the national championship five times.

During the past half-dozen years, North Carolina and Kentucky have jockeyed for the title of "winningest college basketball program in history." With Smith's phenomenal success, UNC overtook the Wildcats in 1991, and a 90-67 win over Pitt on Nov. 29, 1994, made Carolina the first program in history to record 1,600 wins.

UNC led 1,626 to 1,616 entering the 1995-96 season, but Kentucky — which began its program in 1903 and had a seven-year head start — went 34-2 in '96, winning the NCAA title and taking a three-game lead over UNC on the all-time wins list.

A year later, Harp offered Smith the No. 2 assistant's job at Kansas, promising that Smith would be the head coach within five or six years. Smith turned it down, saying he didn't think he could disagree with Harp, whom he still considered his coach.

Still, when McGuire left UNC in August 1961, Smith was not sure he was ready to become a head coach. He and McGuire's wife, Pat, tried to talk McGuire into staying, and for a time, they thought they had convinced him.

By Aug. 4, though, McGuire was gone and Smith was the Tar Heels' new coach.

"Carolina is fortunate in getting Dean Smith as my successor," McGuire said. "He has all the contacts I ever had. Technically, he knows as much basketball as anyone. He will do a fine job."

UNC Athletic Director Chuck Erickson needed a coach who could clean up the school's image.

DAMAGE CONTROL Smith faced a monumental task in his first season. Beset by scandal, handcuffed by scheduling and recruiting limitations, the program was in turmoil, and the administration gave the young coach just one instruction — stay within the rules.

"Smith is a young man on the spot, and he knows it," *News & Observer* sports editor Dick Herbert wrote. "But he also is a man convinced that a sound basketball program is far from wrecked by the de-emphasis."

Smith's first priority was to hold on to as many of McGuire's recruits as he could. Billy Cunningham had enrolled at UNC in December, and three North Carolina products — Ray Respass of Pantego, Bill Brown of Charlotte and Pud Hassell of Beaufort — stayed on.

But in 1961-62, Smith had to rely on holdovers from McGuire's last year, notably seniors Jim Hudock and Donnie Walsh and junior Larry Brown. The Tar Heels won their first two games under their new coach, beating Virginia, 80-46, in Woollen and winning 54-52 at Clemson, but finished 8-9 and lost to South Carolina in the first round of the ACC Tournament. It remains the only losing season in Smith's remarkable coaching career.

TAR HEELS QUIZ

14. Who was the guard who served as the "eyes" for "Blind Bomber" George Glamack on the court?

THE KANGAROO KID The following season, 1962-63, Carolina got a lift, literally, from the spectacular Cunningham. Averaging 22.7 points and an ACC-leading 16.1 rebounds, the sophomore from Brooklyn teamed with Brown and senior Yogi Poteet to lead the Tar Heels to a 15-6 record and third place in the conference.

The 6-foot-5 Cunningham was the epitome of the New York playground player. Long-legged and gawky, his shirt-tail inevitably flapping, he was the last player you'd chose in a pick-up game one observer noted. But once on the court, he was a whirlwind.

"He'd out-jump men six inches his senior," *Charlotte*

Billy Cunningham, the "Kangaroo Kid," led the Atlantic Coast Conference in rebounding for three seasons and was the ACC's scoring leader in his last two years with the Tar Heels.

Observer columnist Bob Quincy said. "He'd drive around the shorties. He'd hit impossible shots with defenders draped over him like vines. He'd let go with a 25-footer when the pace became dull. He constantly filled the basket with 20 points or more against all modes of defense."

Nicknamed the "Kangaroo Kid" as a freshman, Cunningham was Carolina's star attraction for three seasons. He led the ACC in rebounding all three years and was the league's scoring champion his last two years, finishing with career averages of 24.8 points (second all-time at UNC to Rosenbluth's 26.9) and a school-record 15.4 rebounds. He was a first-team All-American in 1964 and '65 and the ACC Player of the Year as a senior.

Unfortunately, the cast surrounding Cunningham wasn't of championship caliber. The Tar Heels were a disappointing 12-12 in 1964 and 15-9 in '65, losing to Duke in the ACC Tournament in '64 and to Wake Forest in '65.

"Billy never really got his full opportunity in college," Smith said later. "I played him out of position because we needed him at center. He never complained. ... He had savvy. A player develops savvy at an early age. You don't teach it. A player with savvy knows instinctively

TAR HEELS QUIZ

15. What UNC football All-American also made the All-Southern Conference basketball team in the same athletic season?

Billy Cunningham was the first Carolina player to top the 1,000-rebound mark. His 1,062 career rebounds rank third on UNC's all-time chart today.

what is required in a situation. Billy always knew."

Cunningham's "savvy" took him to stardom as a player and coach in the NBA. Now a successful businessman, he is part-owner of the NBA's Miami Heat.

TAR HEELS QUIZ

16. How did Horace "Bones" McKinney get his nickname?

HUNG IN EFFIGY The first few years were difficult for Smith. They were difficult, too, for Carolina students and alumni, who had grown used to success under McGuire and weren't bound by the administration's "just play by the rules" dictum.

Bob Lewis, who averaged a spectacular 36.6 points for the freshman team, joined Cunningham in the lineup in 1964-65, yet the Heels still struggled. They were 6-6 when they returned to campus on the night of Jan. 6, 1965, following their fourth straight loss, a 107-85 defeat at Wake Forest.

As the team bus pulled onto South Road near Woollen Gym, the players and coaches were greeted by an effigy of Smith hanging in an oak tree near the gym's entrance.

"A lot of the guys were seething, but Coach Smith was

calm and walked up to the front of the bus," Jim Smithwick, a junior reserve, recalled in the Smith biography. "He said, 'Fellas, you don't have anything to be ashamed of. Don't worry about this kind of thing. Just hold your heads up and walk out of this bus like gentlemen. I don't expect a word out of any of you.' "

But Cunningham, the senior captain, couldn't take it. He pushed through a small crowd of students on hand and, as several teammates joined him, pulled down the effigy.

"It was just so unfair because Coach Smith had done everything he possibly could do as a coach," Cunningham said later. "Everyone was expecting Carolina basketball to be what it had been earlier, without the talent and without being able to recruit. It was almost an impossible situation."

The next day, a Thursday, Smith met privately with each player. On Friday, he cut short a scheduled workout, telling the Tar Heels they didn't need it and calling the

It never was determined who hung the effigy of Dean Smith in the tree near Woollen Gym. A handful of students on the scene denied involvement. One report indicated the effigy was part of a fraternity prank, but nothing was ever proven.

Cunningham led the Tar Heels in scoring for three straight seasons from 1962-64.

abbreviated practice "the best I've ever seen in basketball."

On Saturday, the Tar Heels played at Duke. Cunningham scored 22 points, Lewis had 21, sophomore Tom Gauntlett held Duke star Bob Verga to eight, and the Heels upset the nationally ninth-ranked Blue Devils, 65-62, for Smith's first win over UNC's archrival.

As the '65 season ended, the tide was beginning to turn at Carolina. The Tar Heels won their last seven games and finished 15-9, including a disappointing loss to Wake Forest in the ACC first round.

CARMICHAEL AUDITORIUM

Despite the so-so records, the Tar Heels were drawing capacity crowds, and Woollen Gym, with seating for 5,500, couldn't come close to fulfilling the demand for tickets. Carmichael, with full-court lighting and 8,800 seats, was officially opened on Dec. 4, 1965.

One bank of seats was unfinished for the opener, and only 7,000 fans were allowed in. They got their money's worth.

Lewis hit 14 of 20 shots, scoring 34 points, Miller had 22 points and 16 rebounds, and the Tar Heels shot 63 percent in crushing William & Mary, 82-68.

Carmichael Auditorium was to be the Tar Heels' home for 21 years, until the opening of the Dean E. Smith Center in 1986. In 21 years in "Blue Heaven," Carolina lost just 20 games; their final record was 169-20.

Freshman coach Ken Rosemond (left), Larry Miller (center) and head coach Dean Smith look over plans for Carmichael Auditorium, which opened Dec. 4, 1965.

Cunningham departed for the NBA the next year, to be replaced by Larry Miller, a muscular sophomore from Catasauqua, Pa.

CLASS OF '65 Smith also had begun to accumulate the talent to match the grandeur of the Tar Heels' new home.

Recruiting had not been one of Smith's strengths. As an assistant at Air Force, recruiting consisted of sending out letters to academy candidates. Under McGuire at UNC, recruiting was taken care of by McGuire's New York connections.

Smith, however, was a quick learner. He once credited Duke coach Vic Bubas, whose Blue Devils were the class of the ACC during the period, with showing him the recruiting ropes.

"Bubas was seeing high school stars as juniors and keeping in touch with them every few days," Smith said. "We learned from Vic."

Joe Brown (above) and Gerald Tuttle (below) were among a stellar recruiting class of 1965.

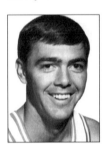

Smith's sincerity and honesty quickly won converts. He lured Lewis, a heavily recruited product of the Washington, D.C., playgrounds, away from Kentucky's Adolph Rupp. And Miller, regarded as the best high school basketball player in the nation in his senior year, picked Carolina from a list of more than 100 suitors.

Then in the spring and summer of 1965, Smith hit paydirt. The Tar Heels' recruiting class of Rusty Clark, Bill Bunting, Dick Grubar, Gerald Tuttle and Joe Brown would set Carolina's course for the next three decades.

GOOD NUMBERS, POOR FINISH Lewis had a phenomenal junior season in 1965-66, leading the ACC in scoring with 27.4 points per game, and Larry Miller was as good as his press clippings, averaging 20.9 points and 10.3 rebounds.

On Dec. 16, 1965, in a 115-80 win over Florida State in Carmichael, Lewis turned in the performance of a lifetime. The 6-foot-3 sharpshooter hit shots from all over, finishing with 49 points to break the UNC single-game record of 47 set by Lennie Rosenbluth. The record still stands.

The season, however, ended disappointingly. Smith had toyed with a delay game throughout the season, using it to protect a lead late in several games, but against Duke in the ACC Tournament semifinals, he elected to stall from the start.

"We had tried to go up and down with them twice during the season and lost," Smith reasoned. "I was surprised when they did not come out and press us."

With walk-on guard John Yokley doing the bulk of the ball handling, Carolina held the ball for the first four minutes. Duke led 7-5 at the half, before the Heels pulled

17. Center John "Hook" Dillon was an All-American in 1946 but lost his starting job in the 1946-47 season. Who replaced Dillon in the lineup?

The L&M Boys, second edition — Bob Lewis (22) and Larry Miller (32) — were an almost-unstoppable combination in the 1965-66 and 1966-67 seasons.

in front by five in the second half.

Steve Vacendak, who scored six points to tie Yokley for scoring honors, saved the favored Devils with a steal and a basket to tie the score at 20 with 2:08 to go. Duke center Mike Lewis' free throw with four seconds remaining was the deciding point in the Blue Devils' 21-20 win.

Duke went on to beat N.C. State in the tournament finals and reached the NCAA Final Four, where it lost to Kentucky in the semifinals. Vacendak, a second-team All-ACC pick that season, was named ACC Tournament MVP and also won ACC Player of the Year, in the only year when the Player of the Year vote was taken after the league tournament. Smith — and many others — argued that ACC Player of the Year honors should have gone to Bob Lewis.

Carmichael Auditorium was named for the Carmichael family of Chapel Hill and Durham, long-time benefactors to the university.

THE FROSH While sellout crowds still were the norm in Carmichael in the '66 season, often the crowds came to watch not the 16-11 varsity team, but the heralded Carolina freshmen.

Led by 6-foot-11 Clark of Fayetteville, 6-9 Bunting of New Bern and guard Grubar of Schenectady, N.Y., the

Tar Babies, coached by Larry Brown, won 12 straight before losing a two-point game at Virginia Tech.

The freshmen finished with a 15-1 mark, leaving Tar Heel fans anxiously awaiting the '66-67 season.

1966-67: OVER THE TOP

Finally, Smith had all the pieces of the puzzle. He had two brilliant one-on-one players in Bob Lewis, a senior, and Larry Miller, a junior. He had size in the 6-11 Rusty Clark and the 6-9 Bill Bunting. He had ball handlers in Dick Grubar and Tuttle. And he had depth, with Joe Brown, Tom Gauntlett, Donnie Moe and Ralph Fletcher on the bench.

With three sophomores (Clark, Bunting and Grubar) in the starting lineup, the Tar Heels weren't given much chance of challenging Duke, the preseason ACC favorite. But Carolina reeled off nine straight wins, including a 64-55 victory at Kentucky, before slipping against Princeton at home, 91-81, on Jan. 2.

By the time UNC met Duke on Jan. 7, the Tar Heels were the favorites. Miller clinched the 59-56 win at Durham with a driving basket and a free throw in the

At 6-11, Rusty Clark provided the size the Tar Heels needed to claim the 1967 ACC title, their first since 1957.

Larry Miller (left), Bob Lewis (center) and Tom Gauntlett hoist the ACC Championship trophy after the Tar Heels' victory over Duke in the 1967 final in Greensboro.

final seconds.

Bob Lewis, who averaged 36.6 points for the freshman team, led the ACC in scoring as a junior, with 27.4 ppg.

Lewis moved from the frontcourt to his natural position at guard in his senior year, and although his scoring average dropped to 18.5, his value as a ball handler and passer more than made up for the points.

"I have scored 27 points a game, and that's a lot," Lewis said during the season. "Now I want to show I can do everything else."

Meanwhile, Miller emerged as the Tar Heels' star, the unshakable go-to guy.

At Wake Forest on Jan. 4, Miller stole the ball at midcourt and hit a twisting, driving shot at the buzzer for a 76-74 Tar Heel win. Against the Deacons in the ACC Tournament semifinals, he scored 29 of his 31 points in the second half, leading a come-from-behind 89-79 victory.

Then in the ACC final, Miller hit 13 of 14 shots, scored 32 points and grabbed 11 rebounds, and Lewis chipped in 26 points to lead the Tar Heels past Duke, 82-73, and give Smith his first ACC championship.

Miller was named tournament MVP, to go along with his ACC Player of the Year award. Smith was voted ACC Coach of the Year, and both Miller and Lewis were selected Helms Foundation All-Americans.

The ACC championship, of course, earned Carolina its first NCAA berth since 1959, and the Tar Heels streaked through the East Regional, avenging an earlier loss by beating Princeton, 78-70, and dispatching Boston College, 96-80.

In the Final Four in Louisville, Ky., the Tar Heels looked forward to meeting mighty UCLA, which had won two of the last three national titles and now featured sophomore star Lew Alcindor. Unfortunately, they overlooked Dayton, led by sharpshooting Don May.

Larry Miller, regarded as the best high school player in the nation his senior year, chose UNC from a list of 100 suitors. As a junior, he became Carolina's star and led the team in scoring average two straight seasons.

May hit 14 straight shots at one point, and the Flyers ended Carolina's title hopes, 76-62.

"Everybody was talking about UCLA, and as hard and as much as we talked about Dayton, I guess we just couldn't get UCLA off our minds," Smith said.

The dejected Heels lost the third-place game to Houston, 84-62, to finish the season 26-6.

SUCCESS AND FRUSTRATION The 1966-67 season was the beginning of a 15-year period of fantastic success — and frustration — for Smith and the Tar Heels.

In the 15-year span through the 1980-81 season, Carolina averaged 25 victories a season, won nine ACC regular-season and eight ACC Tournament titles, played in 11 NCAA Tournaments and in six Final Fours, three times reaching the national championship game.

"A team has to be very good and very, very lucky to win

TAR HEEL OLYMPIANS

Few universities have made a greater contribution to United States Olympic basketball than North Carolina.

Although the sport was introduced into Olympic competition in 1936, it wasn't until 1964 that the Tar Heels first made their presence felt. Since then, however, UNC has been closely intertwined with the USA and its basketball team.

From 1964 through the '96 Games in Atlanta, 12 Tar Heels have made a total of 13 appearances on Olympic basketball teams. Eleven of the 12 played for the United States; the 12th — Henrik Rödl — played for his native Germany in the Barcelona Olympics in 1992.

Chicago Bulls star and former Tar Heel Michael Jordan played on two different U.S. Olympic teams — in 1984 in Los Angeles and as a member of the "Dream Team" in Barcelona in '92 — twice leading the United States to the gold medal.

Few Olympic victories in any sport have rivaled the United States' gold medal during the '76 Games in Montreal, however. The U.S. team, featuring Tar Heel Bobby Jones, had lost to the Russian team in a controversial final in Munich in 1972, the first time in history that a United States men's team had been beaten in Olympic competition. UNC coach Dean Smith was chosen head coach of the Americans in '76, with a mandate to restore the United States to its rightful place as the world's No. 1 basketball power.

"This was the only time I ever felt my only job was to win," Smith said. "In fact, that's what I was told."

Smith's team included four Tar Heels — Phil Ford, Mitch Kupchak, Walter Davis and Tommy LaGarde — and three other ACC players — Kenny Carr of N.C. State, Tate Armstrong of Duke and Steve Sheppard of Maryland. Carolina assistant Bill Guthridge was an assistant coach.

The selections were roundly criticized outside the ACC area, although Smith only set guidelines for the kind of players he wanted. A U.S. Olympic basketball committee made the player selections.

Smith quickly molded the group into a solid team, quarterbacked by Ford and led by Kupchak, Davis, Adrian Dantley of Notre Dame and Quinn Buckner of Indiana.

The United States won the gold rather easily, dispatching Yugoslavia, which earlier had upset the defending champion Russians, in the gold medal game, 95-74.

"I never thought of myself as being terribly patriotic," Smith said. "But when I saw those guys getting their gold medals and when we all clutched each other … well, it was one of those moments most people don't have. There were some tears and some very proud feelings."

Other Tar Heels to play for U.S. Olympic teams were Larry Brown in 1964, Charlie Scott in 1968, Al Wood in 1980, Sam Perkins in 1984 and J.R. Reid in 1988.

the title," Smith said in 1982. From 1966 to 1981, the Tar Heels were always very good, but were never very lucky.

GREAT SCOTT Lewis left UNC after the 1967 season with 1,836 career points, second behind Rosenbluth on Carolina's all-time chart. Smith, though, had another star waiting in the wings.

New York-born Charlie Scott was the first black scholarship athlete at UNC and one of the first in the South. (Perry Wallace entered Vanderbilt in the same year.) Scott wasn't the first black athlete at Carolina; that honor belongs to Edwin Okoroma, a Nigerian who lettered in soccer in 1963, later graduated from the UNC Medical School and became a noted pediatric surgeon at the Children's Hospital in Washington, D.C.

Charlie Scott was a three-time first-team All-ACC player (1968-70) and two-time All-American (1969-70).

Scott was hand-picked by Smith, much as Branch Rickey hand-picked Jackie Robinson to break the color line in major league baseball. Smith had tried to recruit blacks before, including Lou Hudson of Greensboro who went to Minnesota in the early '60s.

Scott attended Laurinburg (N.C.) Institute, where he was valedictorian of his class. He was bright, articulate, though somewhat shy, and tough enough to take the verbal and physical abuse he was sure to face.

It wasn't easy for Scott, but he never flinched. And on the court, he was magnificent.

1967-68: NCAA RUNNERS-UP

The season belonged to Larry Miller, who would win ACC Player of the Year and ACC Tournament MVP honors for the second straight year. Miller averaged 22.4 points and 8.1 rebounds and completed his career with 1,982

Dean Smith with his lineup for the 1967-68 season — (from left) Bill Bunting, Dick Grubar, Rusty Clark, Charlie Scott and Larry Miller.

points, supplanting Bob Lewis as UNC's then-No. 2 all-time scorer. He also had 834 career rebounds, which ranked No. 3, behind Billy Cunningham and Pete Brennan.

With Charlie Scott adding 17.6 points a game and Rusty Clark 15.8, the Heels ripped through the regular season with only an early loss at Vanderbilt. They beat fourth-ranked Kentucky and won the Far West Classic when Miller scored 27 in the second half of the 68-61 championship win over Oregon State, causing OSU coach Paul Velenti to remark, "I've seen teams that couldn't beat Miller and four girls."

The Tar Heels lost their final two regular-season games, one-point decisions to South Carolina and Duke (in two overtimes), but by then, they already had clinched their second ACC regular-season title.

In the ACC Tournament, the Heels beat Wake Forest easily, and then survived a brutal, double-overtime outing against South Carolina, winning 82-79. In the final,

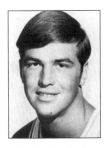

Guard Dick Grubar was named to the ACC's all-tournament team in 1967, '68 and '69.

Rusty Clark was the cornerstone of Smith's great recruiting class of 1965 and the Tar Heels' first dominant big man.

Lee Dedmon was the co-recipient of the Everett N. Case Award as the ACC Tournament MVP in 1971.

N.C. State was no match for Carolina. The usually mild-mannered Clark floored State center Vann Williford, his former high school teammate, with an elbow midway through the second half, and the Tar Heels won, 87-50.

Again, Carolina rolled through the NCAA regional. Clark, with 18 points and 10 rebounds, was brilliant against St. Bonaventure's All-American Bob Lanier in a 91-72 first-round win, and then had 22 points and 17 boards in a 70-66 victory over Davidson to earn East Regional MVP honors.

In the Final Four in Los Angeles, the Tar Heels were determined not to repeat the previous year's mistake of looking ahead to UCLA. Miller scored 20 and Bill Bunting 17, and Carolina won with ease over Ohio State, 80-66.

UCLA was another matter. The Bruins, en route to the second of their seven straight titles, had destroyed Elvin Hayes-led Houston, 101-69, in the other semifinal. In contemplating a final against either UCLA or Houston, Ohio State coach Fred Taylor had offered, "Getting hit by a train or a truck; it doesn't make much difference."

UNC got hit by the train. Lew Alcindor, whom Dean Smith called "the greatest player to ever play the game," scored 34 points and grabbed 16 rebounds as the Bruins prevailed, 78-55.

CADILLAC OF COACHES The 28-4 record and second Final Four appearance earned Smith a new Carolina Blue Cadillac convertible, a gift of appreciation from Carolina fans.

"I'm simply not the Cadillac type," the coach said. "I will accept the gift, though, because I think it is a symbol of the admiration for our players and assistant coaches and all they have accomplished. In that spirit, I will be very proud to drive it."

Not bad for a coach who'd been hung in effigy three years earlier.

18. During Carolina's years in the Southern Conference (1921-53), how many different arenas were sites for the Southern Conference Tournament?

1968-69: THIRD TIME NO CHARM

Larry Miller was gone, but Charlie Scott stepped in to fill the void, leading the team in scoring (22.3) and assists (3.4) and developing into one of UNC's greatest all-around players. Bill Bunting enjoyed his finest season, averaging 18 points and 7.7 rebounds, and both made first-team All-ACC.

Again, the Heels ripped through the regular season, losing only to St. John's in the New York Holiday Festival, to South Carolina and to Duke, and claimed their third straight ACC regular-season title.

The ACC Tournament proved a challenge, but Scott

Charlie Scott drives against St. John's in the Holiday Festival in Madison Square Garden in December 1968. He led the Tar Heels with a scoring average of 22.3 points per game that season.

pulled Carolina through. He scored 23 points in the Tar Heels' come-from-behind 80-72 victory over Wake Forest in the semifinals. In the final, UNC trailed Duke by nine at halftime, before Scott hit 12 of 13 shots in the second half, scoring 28 of his ACC finals-record 40 points, for a 85-74 victory.

With Dick Grubar out with a knee injury, hopes weren't high as Carolina entered the NCAA playoffs. But Scott scored 22 and fed sophomore Lee Dedmon for two

Net-draped Tar Heels surround Dean Smith after Carolina won its third straight ACC Championship in March 1969 in Charlotte.

critical baskets in the closing minute, leading the Heels past Duquesne, 79-78. Against Davidson, the junior poured in 32 and scored the Heels' last 17 points — including a long jump shot at the buzzer — in UNC's 87-85 win.

Carolina's third straight trip to the Final Four, however, proved no more productive than the previous two. With the 6-4 Grubar on crutches on the sideline, the Tar Heels had no answer for Purdue's 6-5 marksman Rick Mount, and the Boilermakers won, 92-65. The disheartened Heels also lost the third-place game to Drake, 104-84, to finish 27-5, ending a brilliant three-year run for Dean Smith's recruiting class of 1965.

After learning under Coach Dean Smith as both a player and assistant coach, Eddie Fogler (above) has gone on to a successful coaching career in the collegiate ranks.

FACING McGUIRE The 1969-70 season was a transition year for North Carolina. The nucleus of three straight ACC championship teams had graduated, leaving Scott, Lee Dedmon and guard Eddie Fogler as the "veterans."

Smith's recruiting efforts, refined and bolstered in 1968 by the addition of assistant coach Bill Guthridge, were now churning out class after class of high-caliber players. Sophomores Dennis Wuycik, Bill Chamberlain and Steve Previs joined the cast in 1969.

Scott was brilliant as a senior, leading the ACC in scoring (27.1 ppg) and earning consensus All-America honors. Smith called him "the best all-around player in the country … a player without a weakness."

But one obstacle stood between the Tar Heels and another ACC championship — South Carolina, coached by Frank McGuire.

McGuire had shifted the terminus of his Underground Railway to Columbia and had built the Gamecocks with street-tough New Yorkers John Roche, Tom Owens, Tom Riker and Bobby Cremins. There was no love lost between the two Carolinas, a situation exacerbated in '69 when McGuire was voted ACC Coach of the Year and Roche Player of the Year. Most Tar Heels felt those honors should have gone to Smith and Scott.

McGuire's Gamecocks beat the Heels twice in the 1970 season, knocking UNC out of a fourth regular-season crown. Then, in the first round of the ACC Tournament, seventh-place Virginia built a big early lead and held off a furious Tar Heel comeback. Scott scored 21 of his 41 points in the last nine minutes, but the Cavs escaped with the 95-93 upset.

N.C. State knocked off South Carolina in the ACC final. The Tar Heels accepted a bid to the National Invitation Tournament and lost to Manhattan 95-90 in the first round to finish 18-9. A North Carolina team hasn't failed to win 20 games in a season since then.

TAR HEELS QUIZ

19. While at St. John's, Frank McGuire also coached baseball. What distinction did he hold in that sport?

1970-71: NIT CHAMPS

With Charlie Scott gone — he left as UNC's No. 2 all-time scorer, with 2,007 points — not much was expected from the Tar Heels in 1970-71. Preseason predictions put the Heels as low as seventh in the eight-team ACC.

After early losses to N.C. State in the inaugural Big Four Tournament in Greensboro and at Utah, the Tar Heels turned things around. Led by Dennis Wuycik, Bill

BIG MAC

Six-foot-10 player Bob McAdoo grew up in Greensboro, was an outstanding athlete at Smith High (he beat Bobby Jones to win the state high jump title as a senior) and a life-long Tar Heel fan. But his SAT scores weren't high enough for acceptance at Carolina, so he went to Vincennes, Ind., where he led the team to the national junior college title. He also planned his return to North Carolina, although Dean Smith had never taken a junior-college transfer and hasn't taken another one since.

Bob McAdoo played only in 1971-72.

In the spring of 1970, Smith had lined up a stellar recruiting class led by Jones and Tom McMillen, a 6-11 center from Mansfield, Pa., who was considered the best prep player in the nation. McMillen announced early that he wanted to come to UNC, but his mother remained adamant that he stay closer to home. His mother won, and in the summer of '70, he enrolled at Maryland.

"At the time, it was

disappointing," Smith said later. "He was the only one who gave his word that he wanted to come here and then did not come. But if we had gotten McMillen, we probably would not have signed McAdoo."

McAdoo, meanwhile, had starred for the United States in the '71 Pan American Games, then returned home to Greensboro to sift through his college offers and wait for a call from Carolina. Nothing came.

Finally, McAdoo's mother called Smith and asked why Carolina wasn't recruiting her son. Smith dispatched assistant coach John Lotz to Greensboro the next day to find out why UNC's letters to McAdoo weren't reaching him. That was all McAdoo needed.

McAdoo had trouble adapting to Smith's intricate offensive and defensive systems. His defensive mistakes contributed to a 89-73 loss at Princeton. His shot selection was questionable (one-for-12) in a 76-74 loss to Duke. And an ill-advised foul late in the game cost the Heels a 79-77 overtime loss at Maryland.

He was, though, a great talent and a quick learner. By the end of the regular season, McAdoo had averaged a team-high 19.5 points and 10.1 rebounds to earn All-America honors.

Chamberlain and a cast of characters including Steve Previs, Lee Dedmon, Dave Chadwick and sophomore George Karl, UNC won 12 of 13 games during one stretch.

Unlike Tar Heel teams of the late '60s, this was an 11-man team. Seniors Chadwick and Dale Gipple, juniors Craig Corson and Kim Huband and sophomore Donn Johnston, and sometimes junior Bill Chambers, played together in practice and often subbed as a unit for starters Wuycik, Chamberlain, Dedmon, Previs and Karl. Originally called the "Firehouse Five," (their own terminology), they were the first "Blue Team."

It didn't matter who was on the court, all these Tar Heels played the same: fighting for rebounds, diving for loose balls and delivering brutal man-to-man defense.

"That's the only way I know how to play," said Karl, the team's emotional leader and now head coach of the NBA's Seattle SuperSonics. "… When you play together, you can win it all. Everybody on our team does something."

On Jan. 4, the two Carolinas met in a grudge match in Carmichael. And in a no-holds-barred battle, the Heels, led by Karl (17 points) and Chamberlain (12 points, 12 rebounds), out-scrapped and out-hustled the heavily favored and nationally second-ranked Gamecocks, 79-64.

North Carolina finished the regular season 20-5, winning another ACC title, and Smith received his third conference Coach of the Year award. Still, the Heels had to face McGuire's Gamecocks once again in the final of the ACC Tournament.

The teams had split in the regular season — the Gamecocks won, 72-66, in Columbia — and UNC had the rubber match won, 51-50, with seconds remaining. However, a jump ball was called when Dedmon blocked a baseline shot by South Carolina's Kevin Joyce, and what happened afterward has never been settled. Dedmon easily controlled the jump, but Joyce said later he got a piece of the ball, deflecting it. Karl said he and Dedmon got their signals crossed and that Dedmon was supposed to tip the ball to him as he broke away from the South Carolina basket.

In any case, Dedmon's tip went straight into the hands of the Gamecocks' Tom Owens standing alone under the basket. Owens laid the ball in to give South Carolina a 52-51 win.

The bitterly disappointed Tar Heels accepted a second straight NIT bid with something to prove. In the opener against Massachusetts, Wuycik blanketed Julius "Dr. J" Erving, while Carolina built a big, early lead and won easily, 90-49. But the Heels lost Wuycik, who suffered a season-ending knee injury, late in the first half.

This, however, was a team of interchangeable parts.

Dennis Wuycik smothered "Dr. J" in UNC's opening win in the NIT. But the Tar Heels had to finish the tournament without Wuycik, who suffered a knee injury.

TAR HEELS QUIZ

20. Frank McGuire coached St. John's in the NCAA championship game in 1950 and UNC in '57. Name the only other coach to take two different teams to the NCAA final game.

Chadwick, Wuycik's replacement, scored 24 points in an 86-79 second-round win over Providence, and Karl scored 21 in a 73-67 victory over Duke in the semifinals.

Chamberlain more than made up for Wuycik's absence in the final, scoring 34 points and winning the MVP award, in an 84-66 win over Georgia Tech.

The 26-6 record and NIT championship, with a team picked to finish seventh in the ACC, were testaments to Smith's abilities as a coach. There was more — lots more — to come.

TAR HEELS QUIZ

21. Who was Harry Gotkin?

1971-72: ANOTHER FINAL FOUR

The heart of the NIT championship team was back in 1971-72, with two major additions. Bobby Jones, an athletic 6-9 player from Charlotte, moved up from the freshman team, and Bob McAdoo, a 6-10 sharpshooter,

Dennis Wuycik won All-America honors in 1971-72, teaming with Bob McAdoo to lead the Tar Heels to ACC regular-season and tournament titles.

George Karl led the 1972-73 Tar Heels with a 17.0 scoring average.

joined the team from Vincennes (Ind.) Junior College.

As a team, the Heels went 26-5 and won ACC regular-season and tournament titles. McAdoo (19.5 points and 10.1 rebounds) and Dennis Wuycik (18.0 points) led the Tar Heels, and both earned All-America honors.

The Heels beat Maryland in the ACC Tournament final, and then roared through the NCAA East Regional, beating South Carolina (92-69), which had withdrawn from the ACC following the '71 season, and Penn (73-59).

At the Final Four in Los Angeles, however, another ambush was waiting. The Tar Heels looked forward to meeting the latest UCLA powerhouse, led by Bill Walton, in the championship, but Florida State played spoiler. The Seminoles led by 23 points with 14 minutes remaining, and although McAdoo fouled out with 13 minutes left, Carolina staged a furious rally to close within four points late in the game. FSU held on, however, for a 79-75 victory. Carolina closed its season with a 105-91 win over Louisville in the consolation game.

THE THOMPSON ERA North Carolina State, led by David Thompson, emerged as an ACC power in 1972-73.

At Carolina, Wuycik, Bill Chamberlain and Steve Previs were gone. And McAdoo, urged by Dean Smith to accept a lucrative offer from the Buffalo Braves, had become the first Tar Heel to leave school early under the NBA's new "hardship" provision. The Greensboro native, the second player taken in the '72 pro draft, was the NBA Rookie of the Year in 1973, enjoyed a stellar pro career and now is an NBA assistant coach.

The Tar Heels, led by George Karl and Jones, lost three times to State in '73 and finished with a 25-8 mark. A first-round loss to Wake Forest in the ACC Tournament again sent the Heels to the NIT, and the scrappy club reached the semifinals before losing to Notre Dame.

The '72-73 season also was the first in which freshmen were eligible under new NCAA rules. Mitch Kupchak was the only freshman to figure prominently in UNC's season. He appeared in all 33 games, averaging 7.7 points and five rebounds.

Mitch Kupchak, a two-time All-American, was the ACC Player of the Year in 1976.

THE COMEBACK Jones enjoyed a stellar senior season with averages of 16.1 points and 9.8 rebounds, and senior Darrell Elston, sophomore Kupchak and freshman Walter Davis emerged as bona fide stars in 1973-74. Still, the results were the same — three losses to N.C. State, a 22-6 record and an early exit from the ACC Tournament following a 105-85 loss to Maryland in the second round.

The NIT appearance that year ended quickly with an 82-71 first-round loss to Purdue.

The season was memorable, however, for one game

— against Duke in Carmichael on March 2.

Fans were heading for the exits and the television crew was wrapping up its regional telecast with 17 seconds left and the Tar Heels trailing the Blue Devils by eight points, 86-78. Jones hit both ends of a one-and-one to cut the deficit to six, but hardly anyone noticed.

Then, the Tar Heel defense forced Duke into a five-second violation on the in-bounds play, and guard John Kuester's drive cut the Devils' lead to four with 13 seconds to go.

Again Duke lost the ball, kicking it out of bounds, and Jones followed up a miss by Ed Stahl to bring the Heels within 86-84 with six seconds to play.

This time, Duke got the ball inbounds, but Kuester immediately fouled Pete Kramer, who missed his free throw. Stahl grabbed the rebound and called timeout with three seconds left.

After the timeout, Kupchak's in-bounds pass found Davis near midcourt. The freshman dribbled twice,

Bobby Jones hit 58 percent of his field goals as a senior in 1973-74.

Bobby Jones (34) did it all for Smith's Tar Heels from 1971-74, but his forte was defense; he was chosen for the NBA All-Defense team nine times in his pro career.

looked for Jones near the basket, found him well-covered, and then launched a desperation 28-footer as the buzzer sounded. The shot banked in to tie the score, 86-86, and the crowd went wild. On the UNC bench, even Coach Smith was dazed; "Is it over?" he asked. "Did we win?"

When order was restored, Duke took a three-point lead early in the overtime. Once again, Carolina rallied and pulled away to win, 96-92, in what ranks as one of college basketball's greatest comebacks.

Walter Davis, an All-ACC performer in 1977, went on to become a six-time NBA All-Star.

FORD POWER The loss of the multi-talented Jones, who, like McAdoo, went on to NBA stardom, was a big one for Carolina in '74-75. Kupchak emerged as a potent inside force, averaging 18.5 points and 10.8 rebounds, Davis continued to show signs of superstardom-to-come and the Tar Heels again confounded the oddsmakers by going 23-8.

The key was a precocious freshman guard named Phil Ford. The Rocky Mount, N.C., product, who had come within a hair's breadth of going to N.C. State, was the perfect practitioner for Smith's Four Corners offense, which the coach used more and more frequently during the next four years. In the Four Corners, a guard operated in the center of the court with the other players positioned in each corner.

"With Phil Ford in the middle, it really wasn't fair when we had the ball," Smith said. "He was that good."

Rocky Mount, N.C., native Phil Ford (12) was so proficient in Dean Smith's Four Corners delay game that it was called the "Ford Corners" during his career at Carolina.

Freshman Phil Ford collects the spoils of victory, winning the MVP award after leading Carolina to the 1975 ACC Tournament title in Greensboro.

Many others — particularly opposing coaches — felt the same way, and Ford's proficiency in the Four Corners, which came to be called the "Ford Corners" in his tenure, intensified the movement toward college basketball's shot clock, which finally was adopted nationwide for the 1985-86 season.

Ford, the first freshman to start his first game under Smith, was part of a UNC youth movement that included sophomores Davis, Tommy LaGarde and Kuester. Brad Hoffman, Stahl and reserve Mickey Bell were the only seniors.

The young team struggled early, losing twice in the Big Four Tournament. But by late February, the Heels were rolling. They ended a string of nine straight losses to Thompson's Wolfpack with a 76-74 win Feb. 25.

Still, Carolina wasn't given much of a chance in the ACC Tournament, with regular-season winner Maryland and defending NCAA champion N.C. State the favorites.

As it turned out, Smith's now-trademark pressure defense and the spectacular ball-handling of Ford carried Carolina to the title.

TAR HEELS QUIZ

22. Who was the first 7-footer to play at Carolina?

In the opener against Wake Forest, the Heels trailed by eight with 54 seconds left, but Ford hit a 20-footer, junior Dave Hanners stole the ball for a Kupchak lay-in and a long Wake inbounds pass grazed the underside of the Greensboro Coliseum scoreboard, setting up Davis' basket with 29 seconds left. After the Deacons missed two one-and-one opportunities, Hoffman canned a 12-footer with two seconds remaining to tie the score, and UNC won 101-100 in overtime.

The next night, Clemson tried to thwart Ford by fouling him. The freshman hit 15 of 18 free throws on his way to 29 points, and the Heels survived another overtime, 76-71.

In the final against N.C. State, Ford ran the Four Corners to perfection. He scored 24 points, Kupchak grabbed 12 rebounds and Davis added 14 points and

Mitch Kupchak (21), here scoring on a tip-in against N.C. State, was the ACC Player of the Year in 1975-76.

harassed Thompson into seven-for-21 shooting in the 70-66 win that gave Carolina its first tournament title since 1972. Ford was voted the tournament MVP and became the first freshman to win the award.

The Tar Heels beat New Mexico State easily in their NCAA opener, but fell behind Syracuse in the East Regional semifinals and lost, 78-76, despite a furious late-game rally. A consolation win over Boston College ended the season.

INJURIES Despite the presence of Ford, Davis, Kupchak and later Mike O'Koren, Al Wood and Dudley Bradley, the Tar Heels were frustrated over the next three years.

With Hoffman and Stahl the only major losses from the '75 team, the Heels went 25-4 in 1975-76 and won the ACC regular season. Kupchak was the conference Player of the Year and a consensus All-American, and both he and Ford made first-team All-ACC.

In the first ACC Tournament played outside the state of North Carolina, sixth-seeded Virginia pulled off a miracle at Landover, Md., and beat the Heels, 67-62, for the championship.

In 1975, however, the NCAA had expanded its postseason field to allow more than one team from a conference. Carolina was the ACC's at-large selection in '76, but the Heels' NCAA stay was short, thanks, in large part, to an injury to Ford.

The sophomore guard had twisted a knee while playing in a pick-up game at home in Rocky Mount the week after the ACC Tournament and was hardly able to walk. Kuester, Ford's backup, was injured (later diagnosed as a broken bone in his foot) in the first half of the Tar Heels' NCAA opener against Alabama. The Crimson Tide won easily, 79-64.

1976-77: RUNNERS-UP ... AGAIN

Mitch Kupchak departed for NBA stardom after the '75-76 season. He completed his career as Carolina's No. 2 all-time rebounder (1,006) and No. 8 scorer (1,611 points). Kupchak's pro playing career was cut short by chronic back problems, and he joined the Los Angeles Lakers' front-office staff. In 1996, he was the Lakers' general manager.

Despite the loss of Kupchak, Carolina again was a veteran team in 1976-77, led by Walter Davis, Phil Ford, Tommy LaGarde and John Kuester and adding freshman Mike O'Koren.

The season was a trying one. LaGarde, a second-team All-ACC pick, was lost with a knee injury in early February. LaGarde's backup, freshman Jeff Wolf,

TAR HEELS QUIZ

23. Who was Kansas' head coach in the '57 NCAA Championship game, and later an assistant coach and basketball administrative assistant under Dean Smith at UNC?

TAR HEELS QUIZ

24. Everyone remembers Michael Jordan's jump shot that provided the winning margin over Georgetown in the 1982 NCAA Championship. But who made the two free throws with six seconds left in the third overtime for the Tar Heels' winning points in the 54-53 win over Kansas in the 1957 final?

Dean Smith talks to his charges during a timeout during a game in the 1976 season. He earned career win No. 300 that year when the Tar Heels defeated Maryland 95-93 in an overtime thriller at Carmichael Auditorium.

TAR HEELS QUIZ

25. What UNC star was nicknamed "The Cobra"?

underwent an appendectomy a week later, and Wolf's backup, freshman Steve Krafcisin, injured a hip.

Still, Carolina kept winning, shaking off a late-January slump to finish the regular season 22-4 and win another ACC title.

The injuries kept coming. Davis broke the index finger on his shooting hand in the ACC Tournament semifinals. Kuester, named the tournament MVP, directed the Four Corners brilliantly after Ford fouled out, leading the Heels to wins over N.C. State and Maryland and to their second ACC Tournament title in three years.

Against all odds, the ailing Tar Heels continued to win — and absorb injuries — in the NCAA Tournament. Ford scored 29 as the Heels rallied from a 14-point deficit to beat Notre Dame on St. Patrick's Day, but the junior star hyperextended his elbow during the game. With Ford playing just 15 minutes, Kuester again took over. He hit 13 of 14 from the foul line and keyed a 79-72 win over Kentucky to earn Carolina's first trip to the Final Four since '72.

In the semifinals in Atlanta, O'Koren scored 31 points and the Tar Heels outran the Runnin' Rebels of Nevada-Las Vegas, 84-83. But the championship seemed predestined for long-time Marquette coach Al McGuire, who had announced his retirement.

The Heels fell behind McGuire's Warriors early, trailed by 12 at one point, then rallied and took a 45-43 lead before going to the Four Corners with about 13 minutes to play. But Carolina couldn't hold it. Guard Butch Lee led Marquette down the stretch, the Warriors hit 23 of 25 free throws — their 92-percent mark the second-highest in NCAA championship history — and the 67-59 victory gave McGuire the title in an emotional farewell.

Still, the job Dean Smith did with an injury-wracked team earned him a 28-5 season and the national coaches' association's Coach of the Year award.

TAR HEELS QUIZ

ANTI-CLIMAX The next two seasons seemed almost anti-climactic. Davis was gone in 1977-78, to become NBA Rookie of the Year, while Ford enjoyed the finest of his four brilliant seasons, finishing second in the ACC in scoring (20.8 ppg), leading the league in assists (5.7 per game) and earning ACC Player of the Year accolades. He was a consensus first-team All-American for the second straight year and was named national Player of the Year.

26. Who was "The Bagman"?

With Ford getting help from O'Koren, freshman Al Wood and a strong supporting cast, Carolina posted a

DAVIS AND FORD

In their five years, three as teammates, Walter Davis and Phil Ford rewrote the record books at Carolina.

Walter Davis (24) was a four-year star for Carolina, earning All-ACC honors in 1976 and 1977.

Ford, who followed Davis as NBA Rookie of the Year in 1979, completed his career with 2,290 points, 753 assists and 163 steals, all UNC records. He remains the Tar Heels' all-time scoring leader, although his career assists total was surpassed by Kenny Smith in 1987. His steal total now ranks 10th all-time.

Davis, with 1,863 career points, was the Tar Heels' No. 4 all-time scorer in 1978 and still ranks eighth on the list. He's also 19th on Carolina's all-time rebounding list (670) and ninth in assists (409).

Davis went on to become a six-time NBA All-Star, retiring in 1992. He's now a television analyst for the Denver Nuggets.

Ford starred for the NBA Kansas City Kings for four seasons, later played for the New York Nets, Milwaukee Bucks and Houston Rockets and retired from pro basketball following an injury in 1985. He returned to Carolina in 1988 as a member of Smith's coaching staff.

23-8 record and won its third straight ACC regular-season title.

The title-clincher came in storybook fashion, against archrival Duke in Ford's final game at Carmichael Auditorium, on Feb. 25,1978. Although injuries had caused both Ford and O'Koren to sit out a 72-67 loss at N.C. State three days earlier, the guard showed no ill effects against the Blue Devils.

In pregame ceremonies to honor Tar Heel seniors Ford, Tom Zaligaris and Geff Crompton, Ford was visibly shaken by a two-minute, standing ovation.

"I told my friends I wasn't going to cry," Ford said.

John Kuester proved a more-than-adequate fill-in for injured Phil Ford in 1977 postseason play, winning MVP awards in the ACC Tournament and the NCAA East Regional.

Phil Ford jumps into the arms of teammate Mike O'Koren after Ford's final game in Carmichael, a 34-point performance that beat Duke and clinched the 1978 ACC regular-season title.

"But a big ol' apple lodged in my throat. I tried to hold it back but I couldn't."

Once the game started, Ford fought back the tears. He hit 13 of 19 shots and eight of 11 free throws, including two with six seconds left to clinch the 87-83 victory, and finished with a career-high 34 points.

"I'm sorry it has ended here," Ford said. "It has been so much fun."

It wasn't ended, not quite. The Heels stumbled through postseason play, with sophomore center Rich Yonakor sidelined by a knee injury, O'Koren playing on a badly swollen ankle and Ford fighting wrist and knee ailments. Not even Ford's 30 points could prevent an 82-77 loss to Wake Forest in the ACC semifinals, and the still-limping Tar Heels' season ended nine days later with a 68-64 loss to San Francisco in the NCAA first round.

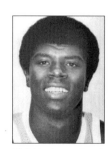

Phil Ford completed his career as UNC's all-time leader in scoring, assists and steals.

1978–present:
Dean Gets His Due

Following the graduations of Walter Davis and Phil Ford, Carolina once again faced a transition. But it's in those periods Dean Smith seems to do his best work, and the 1978-79 and 1979-80 teams are good examples.

The Tar Heels set the tone for the '78-79 season in a Dec. 16 meeting with eventual NCAA champion Michigan State in Carmichael. Early in the contest, Spartan star Earvin "Magic" Johnson was dribbling leisurely near midcourt when Dudley Bradley streaked past, neatly picked Magic's pocket and went in for an uncontested slam-dunk. The Heels upset the Spartans,

Mike O'Koren was Mr. Versatility for Carolina from 1976-80 and ranks among UNC's career leaders in scoring, rebounding and assists.

70-69, Michigan State's only non-conference loss in its 25-6 championship season.

Bradley, dubbed the "Secretary of Defense," set UNC career (190), single-season (97) and game (seven) records for steals that season, spearheading a Carolina defense that got better as the season progressed. The Tar Heels tied Duke, which had been a preseason pick for the national championship, for the ACC regular-season title.

The regular season ended on an odd note when Smith elected to hold the ball for the entire first half and trailed the Blue Devils, 7-0, at halftime. The teams battled to a 40-40 deadlock in the second half of Duke's 47-40 win.

"When North Carolina played the Blue Devils to a 40-40 standoff in the second half, Smith looked like a perfect idiot for his first-half tactics," wrote *Sports Illustrated's* Bruce Newman.

No slowdown was needed when the two teams met in the ACC Tournament final. Bradley harassed the Blue Devils unmercifully while scoring 16 points, Mike O'Koren netted 18, and Carolina won, 71-63.

The season came to an abrupt end March 11, when Pennsylvania upset top-seeded Carolina, 72-71, and St. John's beat No. 2-seed Duke, 75-70, in the NCAA East Regional in Raleigh. In the ACC, the day is remembered as "Black Sunday."

Still, the 23-6 record and ACC title earned Smith his second national Coach of the Year award.

A WORTHY FRESHMAN Seniors O'Koren, Rich Yonakor, Dave Colescott, Jeff Wolf and John Virgil and Al Wood, a junior, provided a veteran nucleus in 1979-80. Wood averaged a team-leading 19 points, the versatile O'Koren averaged 14.7 points and 7.4 rebounds, and both made several All-America teams. But the Heels were never quite the same after early January, when standout freshman James Worthy was lost for the season with a broken ankle.

Carolina lost to Duke in the ACC Tournament semifinals, despite Wood's 32-point effort, and then fell in overtime, 78-61, to a good Texas A&M team in the NCAA Midwest Regional first round in Denton, Texas, to finish 21-8.

1980-81: THE STREAK BEGINS

Carolina was poised to begin a spectacular run in 1980-81. Al Wood was a senior. James Worthy was fully recovered from his broken ankle. Jimmy Black, a junior, was emerging as an effective floor leader. And freshmen Sam Perkins and Matt Doherty strengthened the lineup.

The lanky, long-armed Perkins may have been the key.

"We had lost five seniors the year before," Smith said,

Dudley Bradley was nicknamed the "Secretary of Defense." He led UNC in steals in both the 1977-78 (61) and 1978-79 (91) seasons.

TAR HEELS QUIZ

27. Who was the last player recruited to UNC by Frank McGuire?

Sam Perkins led the Tar Heels in blocked shots for four straight seasons from 1981-84 and holds the school record with 245 rejections.

Al Wood, here driving against Duke, led Carolina to the NCAA Final Four in 1981.

John Brownlee, a member of the Jordan-Peterson recruiting class, was an interesting signee. He was the son of Smith's former college roommate and was signed, some UNC sources say, as a favor to an old friend. Brownlee played very little at Carolina, transferred to Texas after his sophomore year and became a standout for the Longhorns, making the All-Southwest Conference team as a senior.

"but fortunately, Sam Perkins arrived as a freshman even more ready that we anticipated."

Wood scored at an 18.1 clip that season, Perkins (14.9 points, 7.8 rebounds) and Worthy (14.2, 8.4) controlled inside, and the Heels finished second to Virginia, with superstar Ralph Sampson, in the ACC regular season.

The Heels survived a scare from Wake Forest in the ACC Tournament semifinals, winning, 58-57. Then, Carolina survived a 27-point performance by Maryland's Ernie Graham, to beat the Terps, 61-60, for the title.

Victories over Pittsburgh (74-57), Utah (61-56) and Kansas State (82-68) earned the Tar Heels a trip to the Final Four in Philadelphia, where they faced Virginia in the semifinals. Wood took care of the Cavs, scoring 39 in the Heels' 78-65 win. Wood's point total is the highest in NCAA semifinal play and is eighth best for any Final Four game.

Two days later, March 30, an assassination attempt on President Ronald Reagan took the luster off the championship game between the Heels and Indiana. At the suggestion of Hoosiers coach Bob Knight, NCAA officials considered canceling the game and declaring the teams co-champions, but NCAA officials decided to play.

A combination of Carolina ball-handling mistakes and Indiana's aggressive defense, led by Isiah Thomas, decided the outcome early in the second half. The Hoosiers pulled away to win, 63-50.

Carolina finished 29-8, and the season heralded the beginning of a true Golden Age for the Tar Heels. For the next eight years, North Carolina would win at least 27 games each season. And for the next 12 years, Carolina would advance to the NCAA Sweet 16 every season.

1981-82: NATIONAL CHAMPS

UNC's freshman class included the North Carolina prep player of the year, Buzz Peterson of Asheville; guard Lynwood Robinson; big men Warren Martin and John Brownlee; and a late blooming 6-foot-4 forward from Wilmington, N.C., named Michael Jordan.

Carolina was No. 1 in the national preseason rankings in 1982, and the Tar Heels stayed there.

They won 13 straight before losing at home to Wake

Buzz Peterson was the North Carolina High School Player of the Year in 1981, beating out UNC teammate-to-be Michael Jordan, who would become Peterson's college roommate.

Jimmy Black (21), is shown here with teammate Mike O'Koren (31), against Cincinnati during Black's freshman season in 1979. Black would become the veteran backcourt anchor for Carolina's NCAA champions in '82.

MICHAEL JORDAN

In 1981, Michael Jordan was just another name in a talented freshman class for Dean Smith's Tar Heels.

"We had no idea Michael would start coming in as a freshman," Smith said. "He was a high school forward learning to play guard. … He had some great moments and some not so great. But my oh my, did he ever pick up things fast!"

Jordan hadn't even made his high school team as a sophomore at Laney High. He was cut by Coach Cliff Herring in favor of Leroy Smith, one of Jordan's best friends, and according to the legend, Jordan locked himself in his bedroom and cried for the rest of the day.

"I wanted to prove to (Herring) that I was good enough to make the team," Jordan said. So, he spent the next year — as he had spent much of his time since age 10 — on the basketball court. He also grew two inches, to 6-foot-2.

In his junior year, Jordan got off-season help from Herring, who devised dribbling and ball-handling drills for him, even picked him up for 6 a.m. workouts. He averaged 16 points a game for Herring's varsity that season and earned notoriety as "Magic Mike" in the isolated southeastern section of the state.

After growing two more inches, Jordan blossomed as a senior, averaging 26 points and leading Laney to 19 victories and a spot in the North Carolina Class 4-A regional finals. He was a back-to-the-basket power forward with a guard's quickness and an all-state selection, and college recruiters saw the potential there.

Still, Jordan was not heavily recruited. The North Carolina schools — UNC, N.C. State and Duke — showed interest, but few big-time programs outside the state courted him. He chose Carolina over State.

In the summer before entering UNC, Jordan provided a glimpse of what was to come; he scored 30 points — a record that still stands — against the best players in the nation in the annual McDonald's High School All-America Game.

Forest, 55-48, on Jan. 21; Sam Perkins was confined to the student infirmary with a virus and missed the game. The Heels won three more before losing to Sampson's Cavaliers, 74-58, at Virginia on Feb. 3. They would not lose again.

Carolina and Virginia tied for the ACC regular-season title, but the ACC Tournament belonged to the Tar Heels. Jordan scored 18 to lead a 55-39 first-round victory over Georgia Tech, which joined the league in 1980. Then UNC defeated N.C. State, 58-46, to advance to the title game against Virginia.

UNC took an early lead, forcing Virginia to abandon its man-to-man defense. The Cavs' 1-3-1 zone vexed the Tar Heels, and by early in the second half Virginia had the lead. Jordan hit four straight jumpers to regain the lead for UNC, and then Smith went to the Four Corners. The Cavs packed it in, with Sampson hovering near the

Virginia was 22-for-33 for the game in the 1981-82 season, but North Carolina managed a 47-45 victory in the ACC championship matchup.

Still, he was considered just another freshman in the Tar Heels' class headed by Peterson, who had edged Jordan by one vote in The

Michael Jordan was "Magic Mike" as a senior at Wilmington (N.C.) Laney High School in 1980-81.

Associated Press state player-of-the-year balloting.

Early in his freshman year at Chapel Hill, Jordan struggled — with basketball, with classes, with life away from his close-knit family. He once considered leaving Carolina, but was talked out of it by assistant coach Roy Williams.

But if any player ever flowered under Dean Smith's guidance, it was Jordan.

"People underestimate the program that Dean Smith runs," Jordan's father, James, said in Mitchell Krugel's *Jordan: The Man, His Words, His Life.* "He helped Michael realize his athletic ability and hone it. But more important than that, he built character in Michael that took him through his career. I don't think Michael was privileged to any more teaching than anyone else. He had the personality to go with the teaching, and at Carolina he was able to blend the two of them together. ... I think that's what made Michael the player he became."

basket. So, the Heels held the ball.

Jordan's final bucket, with 8:44 left, gave the Tar Heels a 44-41 lead; UNC would not take another shot. Jeff Jones' 20-footer brought the Cavaliers within a point with about 7:30 left, and Carolina's slowdown game became an all-out stall.

The Heels held the ball for more than six minutes. Finally, with less than two minutes left, Virginia gave chase. The Cavs had fouls to give, and only 28 seconds remained when Matt Doherty went to the line with a one-and-one. Doherty hit his first free throw, but missed his second. Virginia, trailing 45-43, rebounded and called timeout with 25 seconds to go. The Cavs never got a shot off. The Heels, also with fouls to waste, fouled Jones twice, running the time down to 13 seconds. And with three seconds left, Cav freshman Jim Miller lost the ball out of bounds. The Heels won, 47-45.

The repercussions of UNC's slowdown against Virginia in the 1981-82 season reached throughout college basketball. "The game had a lot to do with the shot clock being voted in," Dean Smith later said.

CHANGING WITH THE TIMES

The Atlantic Coast Conference participated in NCAA experiments with shot-clock and three-point field goal rules during the 1982-83, 1983-84 and 1984-85 seasons.

In '82-83, the ACC was one of 10 conferences using a 30-second shot clock and a three-point field goal.

Both rules differed from current NCAA rules. The 30-second rule included a provision to turn off the clock in the final four minutes of a game. The three-point line was an arc drawn at a distance of 19 feet from the plane of the backboard.

While the shot clock was retained in 1983-84 and 1984-85, the three-pointer was dropped after the '82-83 season and three-point statistics from that season are not counted in ACC or NCAA records. UNC's leading three-point shooter in the experimental season was Jim Braddock, who hit 43 of 93 attempts (46.9 percent).

In 1983-84, the 45-second shot clock was used on an experimental basis. The provision to cut off the clock in the last four minutes of games remained in effect.

The next season, 1984-85, the 45-second clock was retained, but the four-minute cutoff was eliminated. Instead, the five-second held ball violation was waived. (The five-second "held ball" rule was adopted in 1931, but the penalty was changed in 1983 from a jump ball to loss of possession.)

The grand experiments ended after the 1985 season.

A year later, for the 1985-86 season, the 45-second clock was adopted nationwide. The rule was amended in 1994, reducing the clock to 35 seconds and eliminating the five-second held ball violation.

The three-point field goal was adopted nationally the next year, in 1986-87. The distance was set at 19 feet, 9 inches measured from the center of the basket.

EAST REGIONAL UNC struggled against unheralded James Madison, ranked ninth in the 12-team NCAA East Regional at Charlotte, before slipping by with a 52-50 win. UNC led for the entire second half, but James Madison, working doggedly for high-percentage shots (it shot 56.8 percent from the floor), stayed close and trailed 50-46 with a minute to go. Guard James Fisher was whistled for a charging foul — much disputed by James Madison coach Lou Campanelli — with 52 seconds left, and James Worthy hit two free throws with 34 seconds remaining to seal Carolina's win.

The remaining regional games, at Raleigh, were a comparative breeze. The Heels pulled away to beat Alabama, 74-69, and then downed Villanova, 70-60, to earn Smith his seventh trip to the Final Four.

No coach had ever been to six Final Fours without winning a title. But then no coaches — other than UCLA's John Wooden and Kentucky's Adolph Rupp — had ever put a team in six Final Fours.

In 1982, only John Wooden, Adolph Rupp and Dean Smith had coached teams in six Final Fours. Mike Krzyzewski of Duke joined that group in 1992.

FOR THE COACH The players wanted to win it all for Smith, even though the coach had made his feelings clear the year before.

"I don't feel I've got to win a national title before I end my coaching career," he said. "Sure, we at North Carolina would like to win one. ... But I don't think that's where the emphasis should be. I don't think that's the ultimate in coaching.

"I feel it's much harder to sustain a program than go all the way once. Only three coaches have been able to go to the Final Four as many as five times, whereas more than 30 have won national titles. Which is more difficult?"

If Smith wasn't aching to win a title, though, his players were.

"I'm tired of hearing that Coach Smith can't win the big one," Jimmy Black said before the Heels' semifinal against Houston in New Orleans. "Coach never complains. He never says anything about it, but I'm sure it hurts him because I know it hurts me. That's why we've got to win it for him this time."

TAR HEELS QUIZ

28. What was Coach Dean Smith's nickname as a player at Kansas?

PHI SLAMMA JAMMA The first five minutes against Houston looked like a Carolina highlight film. The Heels hit seven of nine shots, most on fast breaks, and held Houston without a basket to open a 14-0 lead.

However, Smith knew the Cougars, led by Clyde Drexler, Rob Williams and Larry Micheaux and featuring future NBA superstar Hakeem Olajuwon, were too good a team for that kind of pace to continue. Houston came back to tie the score late in the first half, fell behind early in the second period and then rallied again. It took a delay game in the final 7 ½ minutes for Carolina to pull out a 68-63 victory.

GEORGETOWN For the national championship, Carolina faced a deep, talented foe in Georgetown, which featured 7-foot freshman center Patrick Ewing. Smith would also face a close friend in Hoya coach John Thompson, who had been an assistant on the '76 Olympic team that was coached by Smith.

It was one of the most intense, competitive NCAA finals ever played, a classic match between two supremely talented teams directed by two of the game's greatest coaches. And it took a little bit of luck to decide the winner.

Ewing quickly established himself as an intimidating presence in the middle. He was called for goaltending on Carolina's first four shots and another minutes later. Worthy refused to be a victim, however, continually taking the ball to the basket and offsetting the outside marksmanship of Hoya guards Eric Smith and Eric "Sleepy" Floyd, who had been Worthy's hometown high school rival in Gastonia, N.C. Georgetown led 32-31 at halftime.

In the second half, the lead changed hands 13 times, and neither team led by more than four points.

Worthy, who finished with 28, put the Tar Heels in front, 54-53, with two straight baskets. The lead changed hands twice more before Black, who committed one turnover against Georgetown's pressure defense, hit two free throws to give Carolina a three-point lead. Floyd scored to cut the margin to one, but Jordan countered with an audacious drive through the heart of the Hoya defense to put Carolina on top 61-58 with 3:20 left.

Then, Smith went to his delay game.

THE SHOT Ewing, who had 23 points and 11 rebounds, brought Georgetown to 61-60, and after Doherty missed a free throw, Floyd nailed a 12-footer to put the Hoyas in front, 62-61, with 32 seconds remaining. Smith called timeout.

In the Tar Heels' huddle, Smith calmly told his team that there was plenty of time left and reminded them to go to the boards if the shot missed and, if Georgetown got the ball, to foul immediately.

The Hoyas were sure to stay in their 1-3-1 zone defense to prevent Carolina from getting the ball inside to Worthy or Perkins. So, Smith called for a set play to counter the zone, with Black first to look for Worthy or Perkins flashing across the middle, then go to Doherty or, more likely, to freshman Jordan on the opposite side.

As the Tar Heels broke the huddle, Smith looked

TAR HEELS QUIZ

29. Long-time Tar Heel assistant coach Bill Guthridge, like head coach Dean Smith, played in the NCAA Final Four as a collegian. When, and for what school, did Guthridge play?

Freshman Michael Jordan fires "the shot heard 'round the world," giving the Tar Heels a 63-62 win over Georgetown and the 1982 NCAA championship.

directly at the freshman. "Knock it in, Michael," he said.

The play worked exactly as Smith had planned. The Hoyas closed off the middle, and Jordan, who said later he'd dreamed earlier that day of hitting the game-winning shot, popped open on the left side. Black delivered the ball, and the freshman never hesitated.

"I never saw it go through," Jordan said of his 18-foot jumper. "I didn't look. I didn't want to look. Then I knew from the crowd reaction and my teammates' reaction that it went through.

"But there were still eight or 10 seconds left. I had to get downcourt and play defense."

THE PHANTOM PASS Actually, there were 15 seconds left, a lifetime in college basketball. Thompson did not call a timeout, because, he explained later, the Hoyas had a set play for such a situation and he was unsure what defense Smith would employ if given time to reset. The play, similar to UNC's final play, called for sophomore point guard Freddie Brown to get the ball to Ewing in the middle. If the big man was covered, Brown was to fake to Ewing and look for Floyd on the right wing.

Brown took the ball just above the top of the key, with Floyd on his right side. As the sophomore faked the pass to Ewing inside, Floyd broke to the baseline and then cut to the corner, losing his Tar Heel defender.

TAR HEELS QUIZ

30. Name the Greensboro native whom Dean Smith tried to recruit to become the first African-American scholarship player at UNC in the early 1960s?

Michael Jordan, whose basket with 17 seconds left provided the winning points, gets his turn at the nets following UNC's NCAA championship victory over Georgetown.

TAR HEELS QUIZ

31. Phil Ford is the player usually associated with the "Four Corners" offense, but for what UNC guard was the offense originally designed?

Then, inexplicably and without looking, Brown flipped a pass to his right, where Floyd had been a split-second earlier. The ball hit Worthy squarely in the chest.

"I saw him fake inside, then bring it down," Worthy said. "I moved in, then back out. It was instinct, just an instinctive move."

Worthy gathered in the pass, quickly moved upcourt and headed toward the left corner, hoping to dribble away the final seconds. He was caught and fouled by Brown with two seconds remaining.

Worthy, two-for-seven at the foul line in the game, missed both his free throws. But with only two seconds left, Georgetown could manage only a desperation half-court heave by Floyd that fell short.

PANDEMONIUM IN CHAPEL HILL As several thousand Tar Heel fans celebrated on Bourbon Street, 10 times that number painted Chapel Hill in Carolina Blue and white on the night of March 29, 1982.

Nearly 40,000 fans packed the three-block section of Franklin Street, cheering, singing, dancing and celebrating UNC's first national title since 1957. More than 100 police and university security officers patrolled the area, and damage was relatively light — only eight arrests and about 50 minor injuries — although most of the street signs in the area were missing by daybreak. It took five dump trucks to haul away the expended fireworks, toilet paper remnants and empty beer cans.

The Tar Heels returned home the following day, to be greeted by a crowd of more than 25,000 in a reception at Kenan Stadium. The crowd regaled Worthy with shouts of "One more year!" and cheered Jordan with vows of "Three more years, three more years!" neither of which proved to be prophetic.

Martin provided the comedic relief. The 7-foot freshman reserve ambled up to the microphone and sent the crowd into hysterics with his simple statement, "This is a large surprise."

Smith did not attend the celebration.

"He didn't have any other engagements," assistant coach Roy Williams said. "The man made a special effort not to be there. ... There is no doubt in my mind that the reason he did that is because he wanted the players to get the attention. He already had enough; he had the win and the season."

James Worthy, who left UNC after his junior season, is one of two Tar Heels to be the No. 1 overall pick in the NBA draft.

Sam Perkins (left) and James Worthy are all smiles as they show off the Tar Heels' 1977 NCAA championship plaque.

UPS AND DOWNS IN THE MID-'80s

Matt Doherty led the team in assists in 1982-83 and 1983-84.

After going 32-2 and winning the national title, much was expected immediately of North Carolina for the next season, but those plans quickly unraveled. Graduation took Jimmy Black. Then James Worthy, with Dean Smith's blessing, decided to enter the NBA draft.

"I had met in Greensboro with James and his folks," Smith said in his biography. "I had made phone calls to San Diego and Los Angeles. The only thing I do in this sort of thing is to just say to teams, 'If he's available, will you take him?'

"L.A. won the flip (for the No. 1 choice), and the Lakers had promised to draft James if they got the first pick. But we were still nervous when it was announced … because we couldn't be sure until it happened."

The Lakers did pick Worthy, making him the first Tar Heel to be the No. 1 selection in the NBA draft. Worthy played 11 seasons with Los Angeles, appeared in seven NBA All-Star games and helped the Lakers win three NBA titles before retiring in 1994.

What saved the Tar Heels in '83 was the emergence of Michael Jordan, who grew another inch and a half, averaged 20 points and 5.5 rebounds, earned first-team All-ACC honors and was chosen national Player of the Year by *The Sporting News*. Sam Perkins (16.9 points, 9.4 rebounds) and freshman Brad Daugherty (9.3 points, 5.2 rebounds) provided inside strength.

The Heels got off to a slow start, losing their first two games. In the third game of the year, they trailed Tulane, 53-51, and the Green Wave had the ball with four seconds left. But Jordan stole an in-bounds pass, hit a 24-foot jumper at the buzzer and UNC won in three overtimes, 70-68.

Carolina lost again (at Tulsa) a week later, then reeled off 18 straight wins, including a 64-63 victory over second-ranked Virginia on Feb. 10. The Cavaliers, in Ralph Sampson's senior season, led by 16 with eight minutes left, before Jordan rallied Carolina, scoring UNC's last six points.

The only thing that could stop Jordan was foul trouble. The Heels tied Virginia for the ACC regular-season crown, but lost twice to N.C. State, with Jordan fouling out both times. The second loss was a 91-84 overtime decision in the ACC Tournament semifinals. The Wolfpack would go on to win the national title with a Cinderella victory over Houston in Albuquerque, N.M.

Carolina beat James Madison and Ohio State to reach the NCAA East Regional final in Syracuse, N.Y., where it lost to Georgia, 82-77, to finish 28-8.

TAR HEELS QUIZ

32. Name the players who made up Carolina's two sets of "L&M Twins."

THE INJURY JINX The 1983-84 team might have been Carolina's best in terms of sheer talent. Perkins and Matt Doherty were seniors, Jordan was a junior, Daugherty was a sophomore, and freshman Kenny Smith came aboard as the point guard. The bench included junior Buzz Peterson, sophomore Steve Hale and freshmen Joe Wolf and Dave Popson.

Voted No. 1 in the preseason polls, the Tar Heels won 17 games before disaster struck. In a 90-79 win over Louisiana State on Jan. 29, Kenny Smith was fouled from behind on a breakaway, fell hard and broke his left wrist.

Although Hale played well in Smith's absence and Smith returned to the lineup Feb. 29 (playing with a cast on his arm) the Heels weren't the same after that. Still, they lost just once in the regular season — a one-point decision at Arkansas — and finished 14-0 in the ACC.

With Smith nursing his broken wrist and with Daugherty limited by a severely jammed finger, the Tar Heels were upset by Duke in the ACC Tournament semifinals and then beaten by Indiana in the NCAA East Regional second round. They finished 28-3.

Jordan, concluding a brilliant junior year with averages of 19.6 points and 5.3 rebounds, was voted ACC Player of the Year and was consensus national Player of the Year. Perkins, who averaged 17.6 points and 9.6 rebounds, also was a consensus first-team All-American.

Brad Daugherty led the Tar Heels in scoring average and rebounding average from 1984 through 1986.

CLASS OF '84 Perkins, Doherty and Jordan all departed after the 1984 season.

As he does with all his rising seniors, Smith

Sam Perkins completed his four-year career as Carolina's all-time leader in rebounds and its No. 2 career scorer.

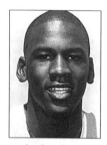

Michael Jordan was proclaimed the greatest pro player ever with the Chicago Bulls, but he was no slouch as a collegian, winning national Player of the Year awards in 1983 and 1984.

investigated Jordan's position in the NBA draft.

"We don't believe Michael's value will ever be greater," Smith said. "Besides, he could get hurt."

"I have Coach Smith to thank for everything," Jordan said in announcing his decision to turn pro. "He made me a better player, he helped me to improve each year, and he made me work to reach my potential. He looked into all of the possibilities involving the NBA draft, then told me he thought it was best if I went ahead and declared hardship. I am lucky to have had a chance to play for Dean Smith."

The Chicago Bulls had the third pick in the '84 draft and used it to take Jordan. Perkins was the fourth player chosen, going to the Dallas Mavericks.

The former teammates met in the NBA Finals in June 1996, when Jordan's Bulls beat Perkins' Seattle SuperSonics four games to two to win their fourth NBA title.

The third member of the class, Doherty, was drafted by Cleveland in the sixth round, but never played in the pros. He's now an assistant coach on the staff of former UNC aide Roy Williams at Kansas.

OVERACHIEVERS Minus Jordan, Perkins and Doherty in 1984-85, the Tar Heels were not ranked in the preseason

Steve Hale (left) was the defensive ringleader for the Tar Heels in 1985 and '86, earning second-team All-ACC honors in '86.

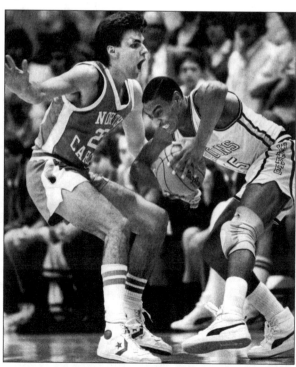

Brad Daugherty hit an amazing 62 percent of his shots in his four-year career and was a consensus All-American in 1986.

Top 20 for the first time since 1981.

However, Daugherty, who averaged 17.3 points and a league-leading 9.7 rebounds, and Kenny Smith, 12.3 points and 6.5 assists, led the Heels to the ACC regular-season title. Georgia Tech beat the Heels in the ACC Tournament final, but Carolina advanced to the NCAA Southeast Regional championship before losing to eventual champion Villanova. The Tar Heels' 27-9 record was better than anyone expected.

With its entire starting lineup returning, more was expected in '85-86. After 21 straight victories, though, injuries hit the Tar Heels hard. Starters Hale and Wolf, and backup center Martin suffered late-season injuries, and Carolina limped to a third-place ACC finish, its lowest since 1966.

Maryland then knocked the ailing Heels out in the

TAR HEELS QUIZ

33. What former UNC player held the single-game scoring record for the American Basketball Association?

first round of the ACC Tournament, marking the first time since 1973 Carolina had failed to reach the semifinals. The Heels recovered to beat Utah and Alabama-Birmingham in the NCAA West Regional, but for the second straight year, were eliminated by the eventual national champion, losing to Louisville, 94-79.

SUCCESS IN '87 The Cleveland Cavaliers selected Daugherty with the No. 1 pick in the 1986 NBA draft, and he went on to become a seven-time NBA All-Star,

Seven-foot Warren Martin (right), a reserve for most of his career, holds two Tar Heel distinctions — he blocked a UNC-record nine shots in a 1986 game against Stanford and he scored the first basket in the Smith Center.

THE SMITH CENTER

The highlight of the '86 season came Saturday, Jan. 18, when the Tar Heels played their first game in their new, 21,444-seat arena.

The 300,000-square foot edifice cost $33.8 million, a sum raised entirely by private donations from 2,362 Carolina supporters over a six-year period. The center, called a "veritable hoops palace" by *The Wall Street Journal*, contains not only basketball facilities, but offices for UNC's athletic administration, meeting rooms, weight rooms and training facilities, a Tar Heel memorabilia room and — added in 1994 — a communications studio. Adjustments to seating since the Center's opening have increased capacity for basketball to 21,572.

There never was a question what to name the place — officially it's the Dean Edwards Smith Center. "If we had named it anything else," one UNC administrator said, "we'd have had a riot."

The final game in Carmichael Auditorium — a 90-79 victory over N.C. State — was played Jan. 4. As the buzzer sounded, Wolfpack Coach Jim Valvano grabbed the basketball and sprinted to the nearest basket for a lay-in.

"I just wanted to be able to say I scored the last basket in Carmichael," the colorful Valvano said.

"He can score the last basket," Smith countered, "as long as I get the assist."

Two weeks later, Warren Martin scored the first basket in the Smith Center, on a pass from Kenny Smith. And the Tar Heels beat Duke, 95-92.

Called a "veritable hoops palace," UNC's Dean E. Smith Center opened for business on Jan. 18, 1986, with the Tar Heels beating archrival Duke, 95-92.

retiring in July 1996 after lingering back problems.

Daugherty was replaced in the Carolina pivot by highly recruited freshman J.R. Reid, who joined veterans Kenny Smith, Wolf, Dave Popson, Jeff Lebo, Curtis Hunter, Ranzino Smith and Steve Bucknall to give the Tar Heels a formidable lineup in 1986-87. Scott Williams, a 6-foot-10 Californian, also joined the cast.

With Kenny Smith, who eclipsed Ford's career assists record during the season and finished with 768, and Wolf leading the way, the Heels lost only twice during the regular season — at UCLA, 89-84, on Dec. 1 and at Notre Dame, 60-58, on Feb. 1. Kenny Smith underwent arthroscopic surgery on his injured left knee Jan. 31 and missed the Notre Dame game. The Heels were unbeaten

Kenny Smith was the Tar Heels' floor leader from 1983 to 1987, breaking Phil Ford's career assists record.

in ACC play for the second time in four years.

N.C. State, however, bushwhacked the Tar Heels in the ACC Tournament final, while Kenny Smith, harassed by the Wolfpack's Kelsey Weems, went three-for-13 from the floor.

Carolina reached the NCAA East Regional final at the Meadowlands, but the Heels couldn't contain the Orangemen's big center, Rony Seikaly, who racked up 26 points. They trailed all the way, pulled within three with a minute to go, but Kenny Smith and Ranzino Smith missed three-pointers and Syracuse won, 79-75. Coach Smith called it "a sad moment" for seniors Kenny Smith, Wolf and Popson.

Joe Wolf earned first-team All-ACC honors as a senior in 1986-87.

The Tar Heels finished 32-4, set a UNC record for highest scoring average (91.3 points per game) and tied the school record for victories set in 1957 and 1982. Kenny Smith, who averaged 16.9 points and 6.1 assists, was named national Player of the Year by *Basketball Times*.

TRANSITION With Smith, Wolf, Popson and Hunter departing, Carolina was due another transition season in 1987-88. As usual, the Tar Heels served notice that not much had changed.

On Nov. 21, the Tar Heels again met Syracuse, in the Hall of Fame Classic at Springfield, Mass. Reid and Bucknall had been suspended for the game, punishment for their involvement in a bar fight in Raleigh in October, and hardly anyone gave UNC a chance against the Orangemen, ranked No. 1 in preseason polls.

The Tar Heels, however, rallied from a 14-point second-half deficit, tied the score on freshman Pete Chilcutt's short jumper with one second to go and upset Syracuse in overtime, 96-93.

UNC went on to win another ACC regular-season title — Coach Smith's 15th — only to be frustrated once again in the league tournament, losing to Duke in the final, 65-61.

Scott Williams helped hold Michigan star Loy Vaught to a single field goal in an NCAA victory in 1988.

The tournament win earned Duke a berth in the NCAA East Regional first round in the Smith Center. Carolina, meanwhile, was shipped out to the NCAA West Regional in Salt Lake City, where it faced high-scoring (110.7 points a game) Loyola Marymount in the second round.

The Tar Heels ran Loyola silly. Thirty-two of Carolina's 49 baskets were dunks or layups, and the Heels shot 79 percent and set all sorts of NCAA records in a 123-97 win.

The Heels moved on to the West semifinals in Seattle, where they faced third-seeded Michigan.

Reid scored 18 points and grabbed eight rebounds, Williams had 19 points and seven rebounds, and the duo

TAR HEELS QUIZ

34. Robert McAdoo is the holder of two Carolina "firsts." What are they?

held Michigan star Loy Vaught to a single field goal in a 78-69 win.

The ride ended two nights later against top-seed Arizona, 70-52.

1988-89: ANOTHER ACC TITLE

This team wasn't one of Dean Smith's best talent-wise. It was a bit slow-footed and not up to the coach's usual standards for field goal marksmanship (52.7 percent). It was, however, deep, experienced and determined.

J.R. Reid, a consensus All-American as a sophomore the year before, missed the first nine games with a foot injury. However, seniors Jeff Lebo and Steve Bucknall along with Kevin Madden, a talented junior who had overcome academic and injury problems, kept Carolina afloat. The Heels lost consecutive games at Clemson and N.C. State in midseason, then lost their last two, to Georgia Tech and

J.R. Reid earned All-America honors in 1988 and '89 before leaving UNC for the pros after his junior season.

Duke, to finish tied for second place in the regular season.

The Tar Heels regained their intensity for the league tournament, easily beating Tech (77-62) and Maryland (88-58) before defeating Duke, 77-74, to give UNC its first ACC Tournament crown since 1982.

For the third time in four years, Carolina had the misfortune of meeting the NCAA champion-to-be in the early rounds. Glen Rice, Rumeal Robinson and Terry Mills sparked Michigan to a 92-87 win in the Southeast Regional semifinals at Lexington, Ky., ending UNC's season at 29-8.

DARK CLOUDS ... Reid left UNC following the '89 season. His career with the Tar Heels had been a rocky one, but Smith, as he has done and continues to do, tested the NBA waters and advised his junior star to enter the draft. Reid was drafted in the first round by the Charlotte Hornets.

Without Reid, the Tar Heels lacked inside power in 1989-90, and the situation worsened when Scott Williams underwent an appendectomy in October and was slowed for the first month. With little inside game and junior Rick Fox the only dependable outside threat, Carolina struggled all year.

The Tar Heels were 17-11 going into the final week of the regular season, when they faced Georgia Tech and Duke, both of whom would reach the NCAA Final Four. Fox hit two free throws with four seconds left to edge the Yellow Jackets, 81-79, at home, and Williams scored 26 points despite a dislocated shoulder. Then, King Rice scored 20 points and handed out eight assists in Durham to lead Carolina over Duke, 87-75, and knock the Blue Devils out of a share of the regular-season title.

The Heels then lost to Virginia in the ACC Tournament first round and slipped into the NCAA's with a 19-12 record.

An 83-70 victory over Southwest Missouri State in the NCAA Midwest first round was the team's 20th win, giving Smith his 20th consecutive season with 20 or more victories. Hardly anyone gave Carolina a chance against top-seeded and No. 1-ranked Oklahoma in the second round.

Smith, in another bit of coaching legerdemain, decided to run with the fast-breaking, high-scoring Sooners, and with a minute left, Carolina trailed by a point, 74-73. Oklahoma's defense, however, was giving the Tar Heels fits, and with 55 seconds to go and the shot clock running down, Fox put up a desperation 25-footer. He nailed it, and the Heels led, 76-74.

The Sooners came right back, and a three-point play with 39 seconds left put Oklahoma ahead, 77-76. With 10 seconds to go, Rice was fouled. He made the first free

Steve Bucknall was a defensive standout for Tar Heel teams from 1987-89. He was a second-team All-ACC selection as a senior.

Rick Fox scored the game-winning basket against No. 1-ranked Oklahoma in the 1990 NCAA Tournament. He went on to earn first-team All-ACC recognition the following season.

Scott Williams was a consistent frontcourt performer for the Tar Heels, leading the team in rebounding in 1989 and '90.

TAR HEELS QUIZ

35. *What three Tar Heel players were teammates on the Ohio state high school championship team from Walnut Ridge High School in Columbus?*

throw to tie it, 77-77, and missed the second, but the rebound was batted around and went out of bounds off the Sooners. Smith called time and on the sidelines called the play, with sophomore guard Hubert Davis to drive the middle and kick the ball out to Fox on the wing.

The play worked perfectly. Davis drove from the left side, drew the Sooner defense to him, then passed to Fox on the right wing. Madden set a perfect screen, and Fox went to the basket, his lay-in kissing off the glass and in just before the buzzer.

"With all the ups and downs this season," Fox said after the 79-77 win, "now it feels like we belong."

Five days later, in Dallas, Arkansas' three-point sharpshooters ended Carolina's season in the regional semifinals, beating the Tar Heels soundly, 96-73.

... SILVER LININGS By late spring, the future looked much, much brighter. Smith's recruiting class was completed in May when 7-footer Eric Montross, Indiana's prep player of the year, agreed to come to Carolina.

Montross' father and grandfather had played at Michigan, and the Indianapolis product had been the No. 1 target for in-state Indiana. His signing with UNC sent shock waves through both Big Ten campuses.

At Carolina, Montross joined four other new Tar Heels — point guard Derrick Phelps of New York, athletic wing Brian Reese from The Bronx, versatile Pat Sullivan of New Jersey and 6-9 Clifford Rozier, a spectacular inside player from Florida.

The new group was a complete, five-man team, with each player considered by scouts as among the best at his position. It was called the greatest single recruiting class of all-time, a designation that would last one year.

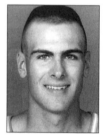

Seven-footer Eric Montross rejected offers from Michigan and Indiana and became an All-American at Carolina.

1991-92: STOPPED BY JAYHAWKS

With seniors Rick Fox, Pete Chilcutt and King Rice, junior Hubert Davis and sophomore George Lynch all back and joined by the five freshmen and 1990 redshirt

Rick Fox, a first-team All-ACC pick that season, clips the nets after Carolina's victory over Duke in the 1991 ACC Tournament finals.

TAR HEELS QUIZ

36. What member of the Tar Heels' 1977 NCAA Final Four team later played in the Final Four for another school?

Kevin Salvadori, Tar Heel fans' hopes were sky-high in 1991. It seemed nothing short of a national title would do, and the Tar Heels almost pulled it off.

Fox averaged 16.9 points and 6.6 rebounds, and Davis, emerging as UNC's best-ever three-point shooter, chipped in 13.3 points.

With Eric Montross (the first of the five freshmen to start — in the third game of the season) and Derrick Phelps in the starting lineup and Brian Reese scoring 12 off the bench, the Heels pounded Iowa State, 118-93, in the Tournament of Champions in Charlotte to begin an 11-game winning streak. Carolina beat eight ranked teams, including Kentucky (rallying from 12 points down in the second half) in that stretch.

Once the ACC season opened, however, Duke proved a nemesis. The Blue Devils beat the Heels, 74-60, at Durham on Jan. 19 and in the Smith Center, 83-77, on March 3 and edged UNC for the regular-season title.

Carolina gained revenge against Duke in the ACC final. Fox was brilliant, with 25 points and six rebounds, earning the MVP award, and the Heels won easily, 96-74.

UNC breezed through the NCAA East Regional, until the final. Temple put up a fight, but Fox and Davis scored 19 points each and the Tar Heels overcame a

King Rice celebrates Carolina's 96-74 victory over Duke in the 1991 ACC Tournament in Charlotte.

31-point effort by Mark Macon to win, 75-72. The five freshmen contributed a total of three points.

Duke also had reached the Final Four, and Tar Heel fans were hoping for a Duke-Carolina rematch. The Blue Devils did their part in the second game, upsetting previously unbeaten Nevada-Las Vegas, 79-77.

The Tar Heels, however, faced a different problem in Kansas, coached by former UNC assistant Roy Williams.

News & Observer columnist Mickey McCarthy called the weekend in Indianapolis "a Love Boat ... with Dean saying the nicest things about Roy and Roy saying the nicest things about Dean."

The Jayhawks ignored the hoopla surrounding the two coaches, and a 9-0 second-half run essentially locked up Kansas' 79-73 win.

37. What Tar Heel holds the record for most points scored in an NCAA Championship semifinal game?

Smith drew two technical fouls, the second resulting in his ejection with 35 seconds remaining and the Jayhawks ahead by four. Quick-tempered official Pete Pavia, who had tossed Oklahoma coach Billy Tubbs in the NIT final four days earlier, assessed both T's.

"I asked Pete three times how much time I had left before I had to put a sub in," said Smith, who was called for being out of the coaches' box as he tried to sub for Fox, who had fouled out. "The game was over. It made no sense to throw me out."

Williams agreed.

"It really was silly," he said. "It was uncalled for."

The coach's ejection brought a sour end to a season that ended just a game short of high expectations.

HUBERT Although Fox was gone and the touted freshmen had played only peripheral roles on the Final Four team in '91, hopes were just as high in '92. Again, it wasn't to be, thanks, in part, to a superlative Duke team on the way to its second straight NCAA championship.

Davis emerged as the Tar Heels' leader. He had been a Tar Heel fan since he was knee-high to his Uncle Walter, the former UNC star, and had come to Chapel Hill although Smith warned him he might never play a minute in Carolina Blue.

Hubert fooled them all, including Smith. He averaged 21.4 points as a senior, made second-team All-ACC and departed as the Tar Heels' No. 15 all-time scorer.

Hubert Davis is the nephew of former UNC player Walter Davis.

Despite the heroics of Davis and the emergence of Lynch as an inside force, '92 was a roller-coaster year. The Heels played brilliantly in beating Houston, coming from 15 points down at halftime to win, 68-65, and then lost in the Smith Center to new ACC member Florida State in the Seminoles' first league game, 86-74, despite Davis' record-tying seven three-pointers. They dominated highly regarded Purdue, 78-50, and then couldn't handle a

Three-point sharpshooter Hubert Davis earned All-ACC Tournament honors in 1991 and '92, leading the Tar Heels to the final in both seasons.

mediocre Notre Dame club, losing 88-76.

In the ACC, the Heels lost twice to N.C. State. In between, they upset No. 1 Duke in a 75-73 barnburner in the Smith Center that left both teams bruised and bloodied, and came from 23 points down to beat Wake Forest, 80-78.

The fabulous freshmen, now sophomores, were beginning to contribute. Montross had 12 points and nine rebounds against Duke, and Phelps harassed Devils' point guard Bobby Hurley into six turnovers and hit the deciding free throws with 44 seconds left. Against Wake, Pat Sullivan's two free throws tied the score with 38 seconds to go, and Reese won it, following up his own missed shot with 10 seconds remaining.

Clifford Rozier was not a contributor. Dissatisfied with his playing time as a freshman, he had transferred to Louisville after the '91 season.

The roller-coaster took a dip after the wins over Duke and the Deacons. Carolina lost four in a row, beat Georgia Tech, and then lost its final regular-season game at Duke, falling 89-77 despite Davis' 35 points.

Dispatched to the Southeast Regional, Carolina eased past Miami (Ohio) and Alabama to reach the Round of 16 for the 12th straight year. Then, Ohio

State's Jimmy Jackson almost single-handedly ended UNC's season, leading a second-half rally and an 80-73 win for the Buckeyes.

The 23-10 record was less than was hoped for.

1992-93: BLUEPRINT FOR A TITLE

North Carolina had lost one of its "titles" before the 1992-93 season began. The year before, its "greatest recruiting class ever" had been eclipsed by Michigan's "Fab Five" freshman class of Juwan Howard, Ray Jackson, Jimmy King, Jalen Rose and Chris Webber. The two groups would become well-acquainted before the '93 season was over.

Unobtrusive off the court, George Lynch was the inspirational leader of Carolina's team in 1992 and 1993.

Henrik Rödl played a key role for the Tar Heels from 1989-93 and was a starter for his native Germany in the '92 Olympic Games.

The Tar Heels' remaining four — Eric Montross, Derrick Phelps, Brian Reese and Pat Sullivan, plus redshirt Kevin Salvadori — now were battle-hardened juniors. Two others — senior George Lynch and sophomore Donald Williams — would play pivotal roles in '93.

Lynch, a lightly regarded recruit four years earlier, had played in the shadow of Rick Fox, Pete Chilcutt, Hubert Davis and Montross, but developed into a relentless rebounder and defender and a deadly short-range scorer. And he was a fearless competitor, a leader.

Lynch took his senior responsibilities seriously. Asked before the '93 season what his job was on the team, Lynch replied simply: "To kick them in the butt when they need it."

Williams, a skinny 6-3 guard, had been Dean Smith's only scholarship recruit two years earlier. Billed as a great outside shooter, Williams floundered as a freshman, averaging 2.2 points while hitting 37.7 percent from the field.

But he had the perfect stroke and a shooter's mentality. "If I miss two or three in a row, I keep shooting," the soft-spoken Williams said early in the season. "Odds are I'll make the next one."

With Williams, Phelps, Montross, Reese and Lynch in the starting lineup, the Heels also had a deep and versatile bench. Sullivan, Salvadori and senior Henrik Rödl, who had started as a junior, each could play two or more positions, 7-foot senior Matt Wenstrom could spell Montross for short stretches, and senior Scott Cherry and freshman Dante Calabria provided reliable backcourt insurance.

The Tar Heels were ready to fulfill expectations.

TAR HEELS QUIZ

38. Name the only Tar Heel ever to lead the ACC in steals in a season.

MEET THE FAB FIVE The Tar Heels started the season on the run, blasting Old Dominion, 119-82, in the Smith Center on Dec.1. Williams scored 21 points, Montross 20, Reese 19, Sullivan 18, and the Heels hit 24 of 28 shots (85.7 percent) in the second half.

The Tar Heels were 7-0 when they went to Hawaii for the Rainbow Classic in late December. An 80-59 breeze over Southwestern Louisiana set up a second-round match with Michigan and its "Fab Five." The Wolverines, ranked No. 1 in the preseason, had lost at Duke on Dec. 5 and slipped to No. 6 in the polls. The Tar Heels were No. 5.

After 39 minutes of trash-talking and chest-thumping, the Wolverines led by a point, 77-76. Phelps drove the

Derrick Phelps squares off against Wake Forest's Randolph Childress in a 1993 meeting in the Smith Center. Phelps holds the UNC career record with 247 steals.

39. What North Carolina native was a star on the Georgetown team that UNC beat to win the 1982 NCAA Championship?

Eric Montross (00) and Brian Reese (31) apply the Carolina defense to Wake Forest's Anthony Tucker during a game in the 1992 ACC Tournament. The Heels advanced to the finals against Duke, but were unable to defend their crown.

middle for a running one-hander that hovered on the rim and fell in, giving Carolina a 78-77 lead with 11 seconds left. Michigan hurried downcourt, and as Montross and Lynch converged on him, King got off an off-balance baseline shot. It missed, but Rose was in perfect position to grab the rebound and put it in. Michigan had won the first round, 79-78.

NO MORE LOSSES Carolina recovered quickly from the loss, pounded host Hawaii, 101-84, the next night, then returned home to win eight more times, running its record to 17-1.

On Jan. 27, the win streak was threatened by Florida State, which held a 65-44 lead with 12 minutes to go. But Carolina outscored the Seminoles 15-0 in a four-minute stretch and further battled to cut the FSU lead to 77-76 with 1:59 left. Lynch then stole a Charlie Ward pass and went in for a dunk to put the Heels ahead.

Lynch's breakaway sent the capacity crowd into hysterics and left FSU star Sam Cassell, who had dubbed

the Tar Heel faithful a "cheese and wine crowd" following the Seminole upset in the Smith Center the year before, shaking his head.

As February rolled around, shooting troubles spelled Carolina's downfall. On Jan. 30 in Winston-Salem, the Demon Deacons shot 60 percent in downing the Tar Heels, 88-62. Four days later at Duke, Carolina's shooting faltered. Williams went three-for-15 and the Tar Heels were a combined two-for-15 from three-point range in an 81-67 loss.

Lynch called a team meeting the next day. After the meeting broke up and as the Heels walked onto the Smith Center floor for practice, Phelps winked at assistant coach Phil Ford.

"We will not lose again," Phelps said. He was almost right.

TOURNAMENT TIME Carolina won its next 11 games, including an 86-76 victory at Florida State on Feb. 27 that virtually sewed up the regular-season title. Reese, healthy after a rash of early season injuries, scored 18 of his career-high 25 in the second half.

The Heels avenged the loss to Wake, beating the Deacons, 83-65, and crushed Duke, 83-69, with Williams scoring 27, to close out the regular season.

With Lynch scoring 22 points and grabbing 15 rebounds in just 28 minutes, Carolina ripped Maryland, 102-66, in the first round of the ACC Tournament.

The Tar Heels' second-round match with Virginia was an odd one — and costly. A fierce snow storm interrupted power to the Charlotte Coliseum, forcing a 27-minute delay in the second half. When play resumed, Carolina pulled away to an easy 74-56 win, but with 1:52 remaining, Phelps was fouled on a breakaway and landed hard on his back.

His injury was diagnosed as a severely bruised tailbone. He would not play in the championship game. Even with Phelps, the Tar Heels would have had trouble with Georgia Tech the following night. Reese scored 24 and Montross had 19 points and a career-high 17 rebounds, but Tech's James Forrest was unstoppable, hitting 11 of 19 shots and scoring 27 points in the Yellow Jackets' 77-75 victory.

ROAD TO NEW ORLEANS Carolina's 28-4 record earned it the No. 1 seed in the NCAA East Regional, and the Tar Heels breezed through the first two games against East Carolina (85-65) and Rhode Island (112-67).

The next two wins didn't come so easily. Carolina overcame an early Arkansas lead, but couldn't shake the pesky Razorbacks until Williams scored on a back-door

40. Who holds the Carolina record for most blocked shots in a game?

Brian Reese recovered from early season injuries to play a key role on the Tar Heels' 1993 championship team.

cut — on a play called by Smith during a timeout — with 42 seconds remaining, giving the Heels an 80-74 win.

Cincinnati proved even tougher two days later. The Bearcats' Nick Van Exel canned five three-pointers in the first 17 minutes, staking Cincy to a 35-24 lead, before Lynch rallied UNC to within a point, 37-36, at halftime. The rest of the game was tight, with Williams settling matters in overtime, nailing a pair of clutch three-pointers. Then the Tar Heels pulled away, 75-68.

KANSAS, AGAIN Carolina was happy to return to New Orleans, where it had won the NCAA title in '82, but not so happy about meeting Kansas and Roy Williams again.

First of all, Williams had expropriated the Tar Heel tradition of spitting in the Mississippi for luck, a tradition he'd started as a Tar Heel assistant in '82. Informed that the Jayhawks' first order of business in New Orleans had been to visit the waterfront to spit in the Big Muddy, Phelps was incensed; "They can't do that," he said. "That's our good-luck charm!"

The Tar Heels led almost all the way against Kansas, trailing only in the opening minutes. The persistent Jayhawks hung in until about three minutes remained, before Donald Williams, who was five-for-seven from three-point range with 25 points, buried them with a pair of treys. Montross scored 23 and Lynch had 14 points and 10 rebounds — his third straight double-double — in the 78-68 win.

Michigan, meanwhile, had to battle for its life, escaping with an 81-78 overtime win against Kentucky.

Roy Williams, who was a UNC assistant coach during the 1982 national championship season, has led his Kansas team to the Final Four twice in the 1990s.

BATTLE ON THE BAYOU In a chance meeting with Duke Coach Mike Krzyzewski in New Orleans, Michigan Coach Steve Fisher had received this advice: "Steve, believe me, the guy you gotta watch for is Lynch. He's the killer. He's a warrior. He's the one."

In the game's opening minutes, Lynch grabbed two rebounds, blocked a shot and drew a charging foul as Carolina jumped in front 9-4. But Webber shook loose for a monster slam, and the Wolverines caught fire. Senior reserve Rob Pelinka hit back-to-back three-pointers — Michigan hadn't made a three-pointer against Kentucky— and the Wolverines led, 23-13.

Smith switched defenses, going from a man-to-man to a 2-3 zone, and the change seemed to confuse the Wolverines. Williams nailed his first three-pointer, igniting a 12-2 UNC run, and then added another with 49 seconds left, giving Carolina a 42-36 lead at halftime.

Two hooks by Montross gave the Heels an eight-point lead early in the second half, but Michigan fought back, mostly on Webber's bullish inside play. The Wolverines

TAR HEELS QUIZ

41. Who scored the first basket in the Dean E. Smith Center?

took the lead on a Howard jumper with 6:58 to play, and then with 5:26 left Rose nailed a three-pointer and Michigan was in front, 65-61.

Williams and King swapped jumpers, and then Williams again brought the Heels back, canning his fifth trey of the night. Montross and Lynch blocked King's baseline move, Reese grabbed the loose ball and fired a long pass to Phelps, whose layup hung on the rim, then fell through to give the Heels the lead, 68-67, with 3:08 left.

King missed an ill-advised three-point try, and Webber, trying to save the rebound, threw the ball right into Williams' hands. Carolina called timeout with 2:28 left.

Twenty seconds later, Lynch hit a short fall-away jumper over Howard for a 70-67 Carolina lead. On the ensuing possession, the Wolverines misfired again. Rose tried to drive through the Tar Heels' zone defense and lost the ball, with Williams coming up with it.

UNC had fouls to give, and Michigan's defense scrambled frantically while the Heels played keep away. With 1:05 left, Webber knocked the ball out of bounds, but on the in-bounds play, Montross slipped away from Howard, took Lynch's pass and slammed it home to put Carolina up, 72-67.

Jackson retaliated with an 18-footer to cut the lead to 72-69, and with 46 seconds left, Fisher called Michigan's last timeout.

TIME OUT! Exactly what Fisher said during that timeout has been debated ever since. But most reports say the Wolverine coach's talk went something like this:

"OK, no timeouts left! Press them! Look for the turnover! If we don't get the ball quickly, we'll have to foul!"

Maybe Webber didn't hear over the noise of the crowd and the bands playing. Or maybe he just wasn't paying attention.

Carolina gave Michigan an opening. Reese took Lynch's in-bounds pass, but stepped on the out-of-bounds line near midcourt with 45 seconds remaining. Rose missed a long three-pointer, but Webber stuffed it back in, cutting the Tar Heels' lead to 72-71 with 36 seconds left.

With 20 seconds left, Michigan's Pelinka fouled Sullivan. The Wolverine senior, obviously having taken some tips from his freshman cohorts, tried to unnerve the Tar Heel junior.

"This is for the national championship, baby," Pelinka said as Sullivan stood at the foul line. "Don't nut up." Sullivan swished his first foul shot for a 73-71 lead.

But Sullivan's second shot hit the back of the rim, and Webber was there to grab it. The big freshman looked dazed for a moment. Lynch applied pressure

TAR HEELS QUIZ

42. *What early '90s Tar Heel All-American listed his post-college ambition as "professional bass fisherman"?*

George Lynch led the Tar Heels in rebounding for three straight seasons from 1991-93. He was the MVP of the NCAA East Regional in '93.

The Tar Heels took center stage in the Louisiana Superdome to celebrate their NCAA championship victory over Michigan.

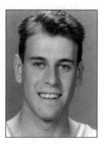

Pat Sullivan's free throw gave UNC a 73-71 lead with 20 seconds remaining in the 1993 NCAA title game.

momentarily, and Webber's pivot foot slid.

"Walk!" Smith screamed, leaping off the Carolina bench. But referee Jim Stupin didn't blow his whistle.

Webber rushed upcourt, past Rose, who was calling for the ball, and into the right corner.

Lynch cut him off. Webber picked up his dribble, and as he did, Phelps also collapsed on him.

Webber had nowhere to go. Hemmed in by Lynch and Phelps, he dragged his foot again — again, no traveling call. Then, with 11 seconds left, Webber called a timeout Michigan didn't have.

Webber said later he thought he heard someone on the bench — maybe reserve Michael Talley — yell for a timeout. Or maybe it was someone in the stands.

"I heard someone say, 'Call the TO. Call the TO,' " Webber said. "It was my fault. I should have known better."

The Tar Heels stood still, momentarily dazed.

"I didn't know at first," said Montross. "Then I looked upcourt and Coach (Bill) Guthridge was jumping up and down. I knew Coach Guthridge knew every stat that was going on. That's when I figured something good had happened."

Williams, named Final Four MVP, drained both the technical free throws, and after Jackson chased him down with eight seconds left, Williams nailed two more foul tosses, giving him 25 points for the night.

Down by six, Rose launched a desperation long shot. Lynch swept the miss off the board — his 10th rebound of the game — and sent the ball to Phelps, who dribbled away the last seconds. The score was 77-71.

"You can call it lucky, or you can call it fortunate," Smith said, "but it still says NCAA championship on it."

CELEBRATION TIME The victory celebration in Chapel Hill on the night of April 5, 1993, dwarfed the one 11 years earlier. More than 8,000 fans packed Carmichael Auditorium to watch on wide-screen television, and when the game ended, they joined a mob of more than 50,000 that poured from downtown pubs to blockade Franklin and Columbia streets on a cold, rainy night.

Town and university security officers had to call for reinforcements from Durham to handle the rowdy crowd, which lit bonfires, shot fireworks, partied and painted everything in sight. There was one serious injury — a fan from Greensboro was struck by a car as he rushed to join the celebration — but damage was relatively light. "The hard part," a member of the cleanup crew said, "is getting this Carolina Blue paint off the walls, street signs and store windows. They even painted the trees."

More than 15,000 fans jammed the Smith Center for an official welcome for the NCAA champions the following day. Just as in 1982, Smith did not attend; he was out of town, supposedly on a recruiting trip.

Donald Williams made a number of big plays in the 1993 national title game, and he wound up with the Final Four MVP trophy to prove it.

1993-94: NO REPEAT

The loss of George Lynch was critical to the Tar Heels. Lynch's leadership and iron will were sorely needed on a team that, while immensely talented, lacked

Eric Montross (00) and Jerry Stackhouse (42) pin N.C. State's Mark Davis in an ACC tilt in 1994. Although the Tar Heels didn't repeat as NCAA champions, they did capture the 1994 ACC Tournament title.

Flamboyant Jerry Stackhouse was selected national Player of the Year by Sports Illustrated *in 1995.*

TAR HEELS QUIZ

43. Hubert Davis, star backcourt performer in the early '80s, also was an accomplished musician. What instrument did Davis play?

the cohesiveness of earlier Dean Smith-coached teams.

Eric Montross, Derrick Phelps, Brian Reese and Kevin Salvadori returned for their final seasons; Pat Sullivan, plagued by a bad back, decided to sit out the year. They were joined by Smith's best recruiting class since '90, featuring three of the nation's best prospects in in-state products Jerry Stackhouse of Kinston and Jeff McInnis of Charlotte, along with Rasheed Wallace from Philadelphia.

The Tar Heels were ranked No. 1 in the nation in the preseason, and they played like it, losing only to Massachusetts, 91-86 in overtime, in the semifinals of the Preseason NIT in building a 12-1 record.

Georgia Tech's James Forrest, who burned the Heels in the ACC Tournament the year before, did it again in Atlanta, scoring 16 of his 22 points in the second half of an 89-69 Georgia Tech upset Jan. 12. Six days later, Virginia's Junior Burrough did the same, scoring 22 as the Cavaliers shocked the Heels, 81-77.

Donald Williams, who had returned from the winter

break with tendinitis in his foot, was ineffective against Tech, going zero-for-eight. At Virginia, he was zero-for-four before suffering a shoulder injury that sidelined him for nearly a month.

The Heels stumbled again in mid-February, losing back-to-back games to Tech (Forrest scored 25) and Clemson, and then shot poorly (22 of 65, 33.8 percent) in a 68-61 loss at Wake Forest. Still, they recovered to beat Duke in the regular-season finale, 87-77, to take a 24-6 mark into the postseason.

After an easy first-round win over Florida State (83-69), Carolina and Wake Forest staged a barnburner in the ACC Tournament semifinals at Charlotte. Randolph Childress scored 21 of his 31 in the second half, and the Deacons led, 81-78, with 11 seconds remaining. Phelps then hit the first of two free throws, missed the second, and scrambled to get his own rebound. He then whipped a cross-court pass to Dante Calabria, whose driving one-hander banked in at the buzzer.

In overtime, a Wake three-pointer tied the score, 84-84, with 39 seconds to go, but Phelps, who finished

TAR HEELS QUIZ

44. Name the two former UNC players who played in the Olympic Games basketball competition in 1992.

Donald Williams, here working against N.C. State's C.C. Harrison, completed his career in 1995 as Carolina's most prolific three-point scorer.

with 12 points and six assists, fed Stackhouse for the winning basket with five seconds left.

DOWN AND OUT The Tar Heels dispatched Virginia in the finals, 73-66, giving Smith his 12th ACC Tournament title. Stackhouse had 14 points and seven rebounds and was named tournament MVP, becoming the third Tar Heel freshman to win the award.

Seeded No. 1 in the East Regional, Carolina eased past Liberty, 71-51, in the NCAA first round, but disaster struck against Boston College in the second round.

The Heels, trailing 42-34 at the half, had pulled within two when Phelps broke away for a layup with 15:53 to go. BC's Danya Adams caught Phelps from behind and sent him crashing to the floor.

The senior point guard suffered a concussion and spent the last 15 minutes of his college career dazed and disoriented on the bench.

The game was tied four times in the final nine minutes, the last at 72-72 with 1:01 to go. The Heels trailed 75-72 and had the ball in the closing seconds, but Wallace, unable to find an open teammate with the last seconds ticking away, launched a long, three-point attempt from the left corner. The only three-point attempt of Wallace's UNC career rimmed out with two seconds remaining.

It was a disappointing end to the season, and certainly a sad finale for the four seniors — Phelps, Montross, Reese and Salvadori. In four seasons in Chapel Hill, the quartet played key roles in 114 victories, two ACC Tournament championships, two Final Fours and one national title.

Derrick Phelps had a tough ending to his career. He suffered a concussion early in the second half of UNC's loss to Boston College in the second round of the 1994 NCAA Tournament.

1994-95: FINAL FOUR, AGAIN

Jerry Stackhouse and Rasheed Wallace had chaffed under Dean Smith's seniors-first system during their freshman season, but those limitations were gone in 1994-95. The two emerged as one of the most potent one-two punches in Carolina history.

Stackhouse averaged 19.2 points and 8.2 rebounds, and Wallace collected 16.6 points and 8.2 rebounds and set a school single-season record for blocked shots (93). Both were voted first-team All-ACC and consensus All-Americans, and *Sports Illustrated* named Stackhouse its national Player of the Year.

Aided by Donald Williams (15.5 ppg), Jeff McInnis (12.4) and Dante Calabria (10.5), the duo led the Tar Heels to nine straight wins and a No. 1 national ranking. The streak ended at N.C. State when Calabria missed the game with a severe ankle sprain and the Wolfpack hit 14 three-pointers in an 80-70 upset.

TAR HEELS QUIZ

45. Who was the first performer to give a concert in the Smith Center?

The Heels reeled off nine more victories, including a classic 102-100 overtime win at Duke (Stackhouse and Wallace scored 25 apiece, and Williams had 24), before an 86-73 loss to hot-shooting Maryland.

Carolina's one major weakness — only average quickness in the backcourt — showed in two late-season losses. Harold Deane burned the Heels for 28 points in a 73-71 Virginia win at Charlottesville, and then Randolph Childress scored 26 points, and Tim Duncan added 25, in a 79-70 Wake Forest upset in the Smith Center. The two losses dropped the Heels into a four-way tie for first place — with Wake, Maryland and Virginia — for ACC regular-season honors.

TOO MUCH CHILDRESS Childress proved a thorn in the Tar Heels' side again in the ACC Tournament. The Heels beat Clemson easily, 78-62, and then Wallace (33 points, six rebounds, five blocked shots) and Maryland's Joe Smith (24 points, 10 rebounds) staged a semifinal duel, with UNC winning 97-92 in overtime.

Childress was simply spectacular in the final. A three-pointer by Stackhouse tied the score 73-73 with 4.5 seconds left and sent the game into overtime.

To open the extra period, the Deacon senior, who

Dante Calabria gives chase to Georgia Tech's Matt Harpring during a 1995 meeting in Atlanta. That same season, Calabria hit eight three-pointers against Florida State to tie the school's single-game record.

Jerry Stackhouse goes inside against Tim Duncan of Wake Forest in the '95 ACC final. The Deacons emerged with an 82-80 decision in overtime, but UNC advanced to its 10th Final Four under Dean Smith.

TAR HEELS QUIZ

46. Since the early 1960s when UNC began featuring seniors on the cover of its basketball media guide, who is the only Tar Heel to appear, as a player, on the cover in two different seasons?

scored all nine of Wake Forest's points in overtime to finish with 37 and earn MVP honors, hit one of his nine three-pointers, and Wake held on to win, 82-80.

HOG HELL Carolina's 21st consecutive NCAA Tournament appearance opened with an 80-70 win over pesky Murray State, and then Pat Sullivan, who had sat out '94 and missed the first 21 games of the '95 season after back surgery, teamed with Williams to key a 71-51 second-round victory over Iowa State.

In the Southeast Regional semifinal, Williams scored 13 first-half points to carry the Heels past Georgetown, 74-64. In the finals, Stackhouse, named the regional MVP, collected 18 points and 12 rebounds in a 74-61 win over top-seeded Kentucky, sending Carolina to its

12th Final Four.

Defending national champ Arkansas proved a bit too quick for Carolina in the semifinal at Seattle. Stackhouse sat out more than eight minutes after suffering a painful thigh bruise in the first half, and the Razorbacks' ferocious defense held the Heels without a field goal for a 10-minute stretch while building an early lead.

Down 69-58 with just 3:34 left, UNC roared back. A Williams three-pointer, a dunk by Stackhouse and free throws by Stackhouse and Wallace brought the Tar Heels within a point, 69-68, with 47 seconds to go.

After a Carolina timeout, however, Calabria fouled Arkansas' Clint McDaniel near midcourt. Calabria, who atoned for a one-for-10 shooting night with nine assists, five rebounds and two steals, had not heard, or had misheard, Smith's admonishment during the timeout for "No fouls!"

"I thought I heard 'foul' in the huddle, then on the floor, I heard 'no fouls,'" Calabria said. "It was instinct. I was just trying to give us a chance to get the ball back."

McDaniel hit both free throws, and Arkansas pulled away, 75-68.

A DOUBLE BLOW Williams completed his career as the most prolific three-point scorer (221 treys) in Carolina history. But the loss of Williams for the '96 season was a minor blow compared to the defection of both Stackhouse and Wallace.

Smith again helped orchestrate the departures; Stackhouse became the third player chosen (by Philadelphia) in the '95 NBA draft, Wallace followed at No. 4 (by Washington). They were the first players to leave UNC after two seasons. The double loss left Carolina with five returning veterans.

"Since freshmen became eligible, I can't remember any team with only five players in its upper three classes," Smith said. "This team will have to work hard on ballhandling, rebounding and defense in order to compete in our league."

With such losses, it seemed highly unlikely that the Tar Heels could keep alive their streaks of 20-win seasons (25) and postseason NCAA appearances (21). However, that kind of reasoning discounted the ingenuity of Smith.

With McInnis and Calabria as the team's leaders, with 7-footer Serge Zwikker in the pivot and with freshmen Antawn Jamison, Ademola Okulaja and Vince Carter playing key roles, Carolina won nine of its first 10 games, losing to third-ranked Villanova, 77-75, in the finals of the Maui Classic.

At the end of January, the Heels were 16-4, ranked

Jerry Stackhouse (above) and Rasheed Wallace (below) both left UNC for the NBA after the 1994-95 season.

TAR HEELS QUIZ

47. Identify the numbers and the players for the five "retired" jerseys hanging in the Smith Center?

Hard-nosed inside play like this against Wake Forest earned All-America honors for Rasheed Wallace in 1995.

TAR HEELS QUIZ

48. How many Dean Smith-coached Tar Heels have been the No. 1 overall pick in the NBA draft?

eighth in The Associated Press poll and battling for the ACC lead.

Smith, however, was concerned that the unexpected early success had created unrealistically high expectations for the remainder of the season. That proved to be the case; the Tar Heels' suspect ballhandling, streaky outside shooting and overall inexperience surfaced, and they lost five of their last nine regular-season games to finish 20-9 overall and third in the league.

A 75-73 loss to Clemson in the first round of the ACC Tournament marked the first time since 1990 that the Tar Heels had failed to reach the championship game.

Sent to Richmond, Va., as the No. 6 seed in the NCAA East Regional, Carolina trailed by as many as 10 points early in its first-round game against New Orleans, but rallied behind McInnis (25 points, 11 assists) to beat the Buccaneers, 83-62. It was the 16th consecutive season in which UNC had won at least one NCAA postseason game.

The season ended, however, in the second round. Despite a 16-point, eight-rebound effort by freshman Jamison, third-seeded Texas Tech eliminated the Tar Heels, 92-73.

Carolina's 21-11 record was remarkable, considering the personnel losses from the year before. McInnis enjoyed a stellar season, averaging a team-best 16.5 points and 5.5 rebounds and making second-team All-ACC.

The rising star, however, was Jamison, a 6-8 jumping jack from Charlotte who averaged 15.1 points, led the ACC in field-goal percentage (.624) and finished third in the league in rebounding (9.7). He was the first Tar Heel to be voted first-team All-ACC as a freshman.

THE FUTURE Smith celebrated his 65th birthday on Feb. 28, 1996, and although he remains in excellent health, the question arose once again about when and how he will retire.

TAR HEELS QUIZ

49. Name the two Tar Heels who have been named MVP of the Final Four.

Antawn Jamison became the first Tar Heels freshman ever to be voted All-ACC as a first-team selection in 1996.

Jeff McInnis led the Heels in scoring (16.5 ppg), assists (170), and steals (38) in the 1995-96 season.

Bill Guthridge (left) has been Dean Smith's right-hand man since joining the Tar Heel coaching staff in 1968. Phil Ford (right) has been an assistant coach at his alma mater since 1988.

He answered the question in an interview in June 1996, and the answer was the same as it has been for a decade.

"What I've said to parents, prospects, everyone is that on Oct. 15 (the opening day of practice) every year, if I'm not excited, then I know that it's time to stop," he said.

With his 851 career victories, Smith is 26 victories shy of breaking the all-time record for college coaching wins held by Adolph Rupp of Kentucky. Earlier, Smith, who disdains personal records of any kind, had hinted that Rupp's total was of no concern to him, leading to speculation that he might quit on the eve of the record.

There had even been speculation that Smith might retire in midseason, handing the Tar Heel reins — temporarily, at least — to long-time assistant Bill Guthridge. Guthridge, after all, has been instrumental in the program's success and has turned down a number of head-coaching job offers in his 29 years at UNC.

Many of Smith's former players — most notably Larry

Brown, Billy Cunningham, Larry Miller, George Karl, James Worthy and Michael Jordan — argued that breaking Rupp's record would be a milestone, not just for the coach, but for the program and for the university. They argued, too, that the title of "winningest coach" should belong to someone of the highest ethical standards, noting that, in Smith's 35 years, the Tar Heel program has never been penalized, or even investigated, by the NCAA, a claim that can't be made for Rupp's 41 seasons at Kentucky.

Smith, apparently, has relented.

"(A reluctance to break Rupp's record) would be the wrong reason to retire, if that were the only reason," Smith said.

Assuming he remains head coach, and assuming Carolina's normal 20- to 25-win pace, Smith should pass Rupp early in the 1997-98 season

Smith insists that, with him or without him, the North Carolina program will continue to prosper, which no doubt is true.

Coaches like Norman and Bo Shepard, Ben Carnevale and Frank McGuire and players like Cartwright Carmichael, Jack Cobb, George Glamack and Lennie Rosenbluth built the Tar Heel tradition. Smith and his legion of All-Americans took the program to new heights.

But the legacy to be left by Smith and all who came before him can't be summed up in a record number of victories or in the number of national titles. While Tar Heels take great pride in those accomplishments, there is an even greater pride in knowing that such success was attained within the rules — in "the right way."

That is the heart of the Carolina basketball tradition. And that will never change.

Dean Smith is on pace to pass Kentucky's Adolph Rupp as the winningest coach in the history of NCAA Division I basketball.

TAR HEELS QUIZ

50. How many Dean Smith teams have been ranked No. 1 in the season's final Associated Press poll?

By the Numbers

The statistics, lists and records that appear in this chapter are taken from the University of North Carolina basketball media guide, which is produced by the UNC Sports Information Office. The records are updated through the 1995-96 season.

YEAR-BY-YEAR RESULTS

Year	Overall W–L	Conf. W–L	Season Finish	Tourn. Finish	Head Coach	Captains
1910-11	7–4				Nat Cartmell	Marvin Ritch
1911-12	4–5				Nat Cartmell	Junius Smith
1912-13	4–7				Nat Cartmell	Ben Edwards
1913-14	10–8				Nat Cartmell	Meb Long
1914-15	6–10				Charles Doak	Meb Long
1915-16	12–6				Charles Doak	John Johnson
1916-17	5–4				Howell Peacock	George Tennent
1917-18	9–3				Howell Peacock	George Tennent
1918-19	9–7				Howell Peacock	Reynolds Cuthbertson
1919-20	7–9				Fred Boye	Billy Carmichael
1920-21	12–8				Fred Boye	Carlyle Shepard
1921-22	15–6	3–3	T 7th	Champion	No Coach	Cartwright Carmichael
1922-23	15–1	5–0	T 1st	Second Round	No Coach	Monk McDonald
1923-24	26–0	7–0	T 1st	Champion	Norman Shepard	Winton Green
1924-25	20–5	8–0	1st	Champion	Monk McDonald	Jack Cobb
1925-26	20–5	7–0	T 1st	Champion	Harlan Sanborn	Bill Dodderer
1926-27	17–7	7–3	8th	Semifinalist	James Ashmore	Bunn Hackney
1927-28	17–2	8–1	T 3rd	Round of 16	James Ashmore	Billy Morris
1928-29	17–8	12–2	2nd	Quarterfinalist	James Ashmore	Rufus Hackney
1929-30	14–11	4–7	16th	Round of 16	James Ashmore	Puny Harper
1930-31	15–9	6–6	T 9th	Quarterfinalist	James Ashmore	Artie Marpet
1931-32	16–5	6–3	T 5th	Finalist	George Shepard	Tom Alexander
1932-33	12–5	5–3	T 5th	Semifinalist	George Shepard	Wilmer Hines
1933-34	18–4	12–2	T 2nd	Semifinalist	George Shepard	Dave McCachren
1934-35	23–2	12–1	1st	Champion	George Shepard	Stewart Aitken
1935-36	21–4	13–3	2nd	Champion	Walter Skidmore	Jim McCachren
1936-37	18–5	14–3	2nd	Finalist	Walter Skidmore	Earl Ruth
1937-38	16–5	13–3	1st	Quarterfinalist	Walter Skidmore	Earl Ruth
1938-39	10–11	8–7	7th	First Round	Walter Skidmore	Bill McCachren
1939-40	23–3	11–2	2nd	Champion	Bill Lange	Ben Dilworth
1940-41	19–9	14–1	1st	Quarterfinalist	Bill Lange	George Glamack
1941-42	14–9	9–5	7th	Quarterfinalist	Bill Lange	Bob Rose
1942-43	12–10	8–9	11th	Didn't Compete	Bill Lange	George McCachren, George Payne
1943-44	17–10	9–1	1st	Finalist	Bill Lange	Game Captains
1944-45	22–6	11–3	4th	Champion	Ben Carnevale	Game Captains
1945-46	30–5	13–1	1st	Semifinalist	Ben Carnevale	Jim Hayworth
1946-47	19–8	10–2	2nd	Finalist	Tom Scott	Jim Hamilton, Jim White
1947-48	20–7	11–4	3rd	Semifinalist	Tom Scott	Bob Paxton
1948-49	20–8	13–5	3rd	Semifinalist	Tom Scott	Dan Nyimicz
1949-50	17–12	13–6	5th	Quarterfinalist	Tom Scott	Nemo Nearman
1950-51	12–15	9–8	9th	Didn't Compete	Tom Scott	Hugo Kappler, Charlie Thorne
1951-52	12–15	8–11	11th	Didn't Compete	Tom Scott	Howard Deasy
1952-53	17–10	15–6	8th	Quarterfinalist	Frank McGuire	Vince Grimaldi, Jack Wallace
1953-54	11–10	5–6	5th	Quarterfinalist	Frank McGuire	Game Captains
1954-55	10–11	8–6	T 4th	Quarterfinalist	Frank McGuire	Al Lifson, Paul Likins
1955-56	18–5	11–3	T 1st	Semifinalist	Frank McGuire	Jerry Vayda
1956-57	32–0	14–0	1st	Champion	Frank McGuire	Lennie Rosenbluth
1957-58	19–7	10–4	T 2nd	Finalist	Frank McGuire	Pete Brennan
1958-59	20–5	12–2	T 1st	Finalist	Frank McGuire	Danny Lotz
1959-60	18–6	12–2	T 1st	Semifinalist	Frank McGuire	Harvey Salz
1960-61	19–4	12–2	1st	Didn't Compete	Frank McGuire	Doug Moe, York Larese
1961-62	8–9	7–7	T 4th	Quarterfinalist	Dean Smith	Jim Hudock
1962-63	15–6	10–4	3rd	Semifinalist	Dean Smith	Larry Brown, Yogi Poteet
1963-64	12–12	6–8	5th	Semifinalist	Dean Smith	Mike Cooke, Charlie Shaffer
1964-65	15–9	10–4	T 2nd	Quarterfinalist	Dean Smith	Billy Cunningham
1965-66	16–11	8–6	T 3rd	Semifinalist	Dean Smith	Bob Bennett, John Yokley
1966-67	26–6	12–2	1st	Champion	Dean Smith	Tom Gauntlett, Bob Lewis

Year	Overall W–L	Conf. W–L	Season Finish	Tourn. Finish	Head Coach	Captains
1967-68	28–4	12–2	1st	Champion	Dean Smith	Larry Miller
1968-69	27–5	12–2	1st	Champion	Dean Smith	Joe Brown, Bill Bunting, Rusty Clark, Dick Grubar, Gerald Tuttle
1969-70	18–9	9–5	T 2nd	Quarterfinalist	Dean Smith	Jim Delany, Eddie Fogler, Charlie Scott
1970-71	26–6	11–3	1st	Finalist	Dean Smith	Lee Dedmon, Dale Gipple
1971-72	26–5	9–3	1st	Champion	Dean Smith	Steve Previs, Dennis Wuycik
1972-73	25–8	8–4	2nd	First Round	Dean Smith	Donn Johnston, George Karl
1973-74	22–6	9–3	T 2nd	Semifinalist	Dean Smith	Darrell Elston, Bobby Jones
1974-75	23–8	8–4	T 2nd	Champion	Dean Smith	Mickey Bell, Brad Hoffman, Ed Stahl
1975-76	25–4	11–1	1st	Finalist	Dean Smith	Bill Chambers, Dave Hanners, Mitch Kupchak
1976-77	28–5	9–3	1st	Champion	Dean Smith	Bruce Buckley, Woody Coley, Walter Davis, John Kuester, Tommy LaGarde
1977-78	23–8	9–3	1st	Semifinalist	Dean Smith	Phil Ford, Tom Zaliagiris
1978-79	23–6	9–3	T 1st	Champion	Dean Smith	Dudley Bradley, Ged Doughton
1979-80	21–8	9–5	T 2nd	Semifinalist	Dean Smith	Dave Colescott, Mike O'Koren, John Virgill, Jeff Wolf, Rich Yonakor
1980-81	29–8	10–4	2nd	Champion	Dean Smith	Pete Budko, Eric Kenny, Mike Pepper, Al Wood
1981-82	32–2	12–2	T 1st	Champion	Dean Smith	Jeb Barlow, Jimmy Black, Chris Brust
1982-83	28–8	12–2	T 1st	Semifinalist	Dean Smith	Jim Braddock
1983-84	28–3	14–0	1st	Semifinalist	Dean Smith	Matt Doherty, Cecil Exum, Sam Perkins
1984-85	27–9	9–5	T 1st	Finalist	Dean Smith	Buzz Peterson
1985-86	28–6	10–4	3rd	Quarterfinalist	Dean Smith	Brad Daugherty, Steve Hale
1986-87	32–4	14–0	1st	Finalist	Dean Smith	Kenny Smith, Joe Wolf
1987-88	27–7	11–3	1st	Finalist	Dean Smith	Joe Jenkins, Ranzino Smith
1988-89	29–8	9–5	T 2nd	Champion	Dean Smith	Steve Bucknall, Jeff Lebo
1989-90	21–13	8–6	T 3rd	Quarterfinalist	Dean Smith	Kevin Madden, Scott Williams
1990-91	29–6	10–4	2nd	Champion	Dean Smith	Pete Chilcutt, Rick Fox, King Rice
1991-92	23–10	9–7	3rd	Finalist	Dean Smith	Hubert Davis
1992-93	34–4	14–2	1st	Finalist	Dean Smith	George Lynch, Henrik Rödl
1993-94	28-7	11-5	2nd	Champion	Dean Smith	Eric Montross, Derrick Phelps
1994-95	28-6	12-4	T 1st	Finalist	Dean Smith	Pearce Landry, Pat Sullivan, Donald Williams
1995-96	21-11	10-6	3rd	Quarterfinalist	Dean Smith	Dante Calabria

Southern Conference Totals: 304–111 (.733); 9 Regular–Season Titles; 8 Tournament Championships
ACC Totals: 437–156 (.737); 22 Regular-Season Titles; 13 Tournament Championships
Overall Totals: 1,647–588 (.737)

COACHING RECORDS

Years	Name	Seasons	Won	Lost	Pct.
1911-14	Nat Cartmell	4	25	24	.510
1915-16	Charles Doak	2	18	16	.529
1917-19	Howell Peacock	3	23	14	.622
1920-21	Fred Boye	2	19	17	.528
1922-23	No Coach	2	30	7	.811
1924	Norman Shepard	1	26	0	1.000
1925	Monk McDonald	1	20	5	.800
1926	Harlan Sanborn	1	20	5	.800
1927-31	James Ashmore	5	80	37	.684
1932-35	George Shepard	4	69	16	.812
1936-39	Walter Skidmore	4	65	25	.722
1940-44	Bill Lange	5	85	41	.675
1945-46	Ben Carnevale	2	52	11	.825
1947-52	Tom Scott	6	100	65	.606
1953-61	Frank McGuire	9	164	58	.739
1962-96	Dean Smith	35	851	247	.775
Totals			**1,647**	**588**	**.737**

NATIONAL CHAMPIONSHIP TEAMS

1923-24	Norman Shepard 26-0, Helms Foundation
1956-57	Frank McGuire 32-0, NCAA (def. Kansas, 54-53 in 3 OT)
1981-82	Dean Smith 32-2, NCAA (def. Georgetown, 63-62)
1992-93	Dean Smith 34-4, NCAA (def. Michigan, 77-71)

MOST NCAA FINAL FOUR APPEARANCES BY HEAD COACH

(through 1995-96)

Name (School)	Appearances
John Wooden (UCLA)	12
Dean Smith (North Carolina)	10
Mike Krzyzewski (Duke)	7
Adolph Rupp (Kentucky)	6
Denny Crum (Louisville)	6
Guy Lewis (Houston)	5
Bob Knight (Indiana)	5

TEAM RECORDS

MOST POINTS SCORED, SEASON

3,331 in 1988–89
3,285 in 1986–87
3,272 in 1992–93
3,067 in 1990–91
2,996 in 1993–94

HIGHEST SCORING AVERAGE PER GAME, SEASON

91.3 in 1986–87 (3,285 points in 36 games)
90.0 in 1988–89 (3,331 points in 37 games)
89.1 in 1971–72 (2,762 points in 31 games)
88.9 in 1968–69 (2,844 points in 32 games)
88.9 in 1969–70 (2,399 points in 27 games)

HIGHEST AVERAGE SCORING MARGIN, SEASON

17.8 points in 1992–93 (86.1–68.3)
17.7 points in 1971–72 (89.1–71.4)
17.6 points in 1985–86 (86.6–69.0)
17.5 points in 1944–45 (53.0–35.5)
16.5 points in 1945–46 (56.3–39.8)

MOST POINTS ALLOWED, SEASON

2,949 in 1988–89
2,695 in 1986–87
2,650 in 1989–90
2,596 in 1992–93
2,533 in 1993–94

HIGHEST SCORING AVE. PER GAME ALLOWED, SEASON

79.7 in 1988–89 (2,949 points in 37 games)
78.8 in 1969–70 (2,128 points in 27 games)
78.0 in 1974–75 (2,417 points in 31 games)
77.9 in 1989–90 (2,650 points in 34 games)
77.6 in 1964–65 (1,862 points in 24 games)

MOST FIELD GOALS MADE, SEASON

1,238 in 1986–87
1,228 in 1988–89
1,219 in 1992–93
1,197 in 1985–86
1,150 in 1972–73

MOST FIELD GOAL ATTEMPTS, SEASON

2,407 in 1992–93
2,328 in 1988–89
2,304 in 1986–87
2,261 in 1967–68
2,257 in 1990–91

HIGHEST FIELD GOAL PERCENTAGE, SEASON

.559 in 1985–86 (1,197 of 2,140)
.543 in 1983–84 (966 of 1,779)
.540 in 1984–85 (1,039 of 1,925)
.537 in 1976–77 (1,054 of 1,961)
.537 in 1986–87 (1,238 of 2,304)

MOST FREE THROWS MADE, SEASON

817 in 1956–57
700 in 1971–72
689 in 1988–89
686 in 1970–71
670 in 1993–94

MOST FREE THROW ATTEMPTS, SEASON

1,167 in 1956–57
1,108 in 1993–94
950 in 1988–89
943 in 1992–93
942 in 1971–72

HIGHEST FREE THROW PERCENTAGE, SEASON

.783 in 1983–84 (551 of 704)
.761 in 1984–85 (569 of 748)
.758 in 1959–60 (542 of 715)
.751 in 1975–76 (537 of 715)
.746 in 1976–77 (651 of 873)

MOST THREE–POINT FIELD GOALS MADE, SEASON

266 in 1994–95
235 in 1995–96
213 in 1986–87
195 in 1989–90
192 in 1990–91

MOST THREE–POINT FIELD GOAL ATTEMPTS, SEASON

648 in 1994–95
593 in 1995–96
519 in 1989–90
488 in 1986–87
483 in 1990–91

HIGHEST 3–POINT FIELD GOAL PERCENTAGE, SEASON

.437 in 1982–83 (132 of 302)
.436 in 1986–87 (213 of 488)
.430 in 1987–88 (169 of 393)
.410 in 1994–95 (266 of 648)
.398 in 1990–91 (192 of 483)

MOST REBOUNDS, SEASON

1,561 in 1992–93
1,531 in 1993–94
1,511 in 1967–68
1,505 in 1966–67
1,495 in 1956–57

HIGHEST REBOUNDING AVERAGE PER GAME, SEASON

49.9 in 1960–61 (1,148 rebounds in 23 games)
48.8 in 1963–64 (1,171 rebounds in 24 games)
48.1 in 1955–56 (1,106 rebounds in 23 games)
47.2 in 1967–68 (1,511 rebounds in 32 games)
47.0 in 1966–67 (1,505 rebounds in 32 games)

MOST ASSISTS, SEASON

855 in 1972–73
800 in 1985–86
788 in 1988–89
782 in 1986–87
702 in 1984–85

HIGHEST ASSIST AVERAGE PER GAME, SEASON

25.9 in 1972–73 (855 assists in 33 games)

MOST BLOCKED SHOTS, SEASON

219 in 1993-94

MOST STEALS, SEASON

357 in 1992–93

MOST POINTS SCORED, GAME

129 vs. VMI, Dec. 17, 1994
129 vs. Manhattan, Dec. 27, 1985
128 vs. Dartmouth, Dec. 5, 1972
127 vs. Richmond, Dec. 8, 1965
127 vs. Rice, Dec. 2, 1971

MOST FIELD GOALS MADE, GAME

57 vs. Manhattan, Dec. 27, 1985 (57 of 78 attempts)

MOST FIELD GOALS ATTEMPTS, GAME

100 vs. Virginia, Feb. 6, 1968

HIGHEST FIELD GOAL PERCENTAGE, GAME
.790 vs. Loyola Marymount, Mar. 19, 1988 (49 of 62 attempts)

HIGHEST FIELD GOAL PERCENTAGE FOR A HALF, GAME
.941 vs. Virginia, Jan. 7, 1978 (16 of 17, 2nd half)

MOST FREE THROWS MADE, GAME
43 vs. N.C. State, Jan. 15, 1957

MOST FREE THROW ATTEMPTS, GAME
59 vs. Clemson, Jan. 14, 1959

MOST THREE–POINT FIELD GOALS MADE, GAME
17 vs. Florida State, Jan. 25, 1995 (17 of 25 attempts)

MOST THREE–POINT FIELD GOAL ATTEMPTS, GAME
31 vs. Florida State, Feb. 24, 1996 (14 of 31 attempts)

HIGHEST THREE–POINT FIELD GOAL PERCENTAGE, GAME
.889 vs. Stetson, Dec. 3, 1986 (8 of 9 attempts)

MOST REBOUNDS, GAME
73 vs. Tulane, Dec. 10, 1964

MOST OFFENSIVE REBOUNDS, GAME
32 vs. Pittsburgh, Dec. 20, 1993

MOST DEFENSIVE REBOUNDS, GAME
47 vs. Loyola Marymount, Mar. 19, 1988

MOST ASSISTS, GAME
41 vs. Manhattan, Dec. 27, 1985

MOST BLOCKED SHOTS, GAME
18 vs. Stanford, Dec. 20, 1985

MOST TURNOVERS, GAME
34 vs. N.C. State, Feb. 15, 1966

FEWEST TURNOVERS, GAME
3 vs. Duke, Feb. 26, 1977
3 vs. Duke, Feb 24, 1979
3 vs. Virginia, Mar. 7, 1982

INDIVIDUAL RECORDS

MOST POINTS SCORED, GAME
49	Bob Lewis vs. Florida State, Dec. 16, 1965
48	Billy Cunningham vs. Tulane, Dec. 10, 1964
47	Lennie Rosenbluth vs. Furman, Dec. 3, 1956
45	George Glamack vs. Clemson, Feb. 10, 1941
45	Lennie Rosenbluth vs. Clemson, Jan. 14, 1956
45	Lennie Rosenbluth vs. William & Mary, Feb. 7, 1956
45	Lennie Rosenbluth vs. Clemson, March 7, 1957

MOST POINTS SCORED, SEASON
895	Lennie Rosenbluth, 1956–57
740	Bob Lewis, 1965–66
731	Charlie Scott, 1969–70
721	Michael Jordan, 1982–83
717	Larry Miller, 1967–68

MOST POINTS SCORED, CAREER
2,290	Phil Ford, 1974–78
2,145	Sam Perkins, 1980–84
2,045	Lennie Rosenbluth, 1954–57
2,015	Al Wood, 1977–81
2,007	Charlie Scott, 1967–70

AVERAGE POINTS PER GAME, SEASON
28.0	Lennie Rosenbluth, 1956–57 (895 points in 32 games)
27.4	Bob Lewis, 1965–66
27.1	Charlie Scott, 1969–70
26.7	Lennie Rosenbluth, 1955–56
26.0	Billy Cunningham, 1963–64

AVERAGE POINTS PER GAME, CAREER
26.9	Lennie Rosenbluth, 1954–57 (2,045 points in 76 games)
24.8	Billy Cunningham, 1962–65
22.1	Bob Lewis, 1964–67
22.1	Charlie Scott, 1967–70
22.0	Larry Miller, 1965–68

MOST FIELD GOALS MADE, GAME
| 21 | Billy Cunningham vs. Tulane, Dec. 10, 1964 |

MOST FIELD GOALS MADE, SEASON
305	Lennie Rosenbluth, 1956–57
290	Charlie Scott, 1968–69
284	Brad Daugherty, 1985–86
282	Michael Jordan, 1982–83
281	Charlie Scott, 1969–70

MOST FIELD GOALS MADE, CAREER
865	Phil Ford, 1974–78
825	Al Wood, 1977–81
786	Sam Perkins, 1980–84
765	Larry Miller, 1965–68
760	Brad Daugherty, 1982–86

MOST FIELD GOALS ATTEMPTED, SEASON
631	Lennie Rosenbluth, 1956–57
611	Charlie Scott, 1969–70
577	Charlie Scott, 1968–69
553	Larry Miller, 1966–67
545	Larry Miller, 1967–68

MOST FIELD GOALS ATTEMPTED, CAREER
| 1,678 | Charlie Scott, 1967–70 |

HIGHEST FIELD GOAL PERCENTAGE, GAME
(Minimum 10 made)
| 1.000 | Brad Daugherty vs. UCLA, Nov. 24, 1985 (13 of 13); Scott Williams vs. Virginia, Jan. 13, 1990 (12 of 12); Jeff McInnis vs. Cincinnati, Dec. 3, 1994 (10 of 10) |

HIGHEST FIELD GOAL PERCENTAGE, SEASON
.668	Bobby Jones, 1971–72 (127 of 190 attempts)
.654	Rasheed Wallace, 1994-95
.648	Brad Daugherty, 1985–86
.643	Mike O'Koren, 1977–78
.626	Sam Perkins, 1980–81

HIGHEST FIELD GOAL PERCENTAGE, CAREER
.635	Rasheed Wallace, 1993-95 (377 of 594 attempts)
.620	Brad Daugherty, 1982–86
.608	Bobby Jones, 1971–74
.601	J.R. Reid, 1986–89
.594	Warren Martin, 1981–86

MOST THREE–POINT FIELD GOALS MADE, GAME

8	Hubert Davis vs. Florida State, Feb. 27, 1992
8	Dante Calabria vs. Florida State, Jan. 25, 1995
8	Jeff McInnis vs. Clemson, Feb. 14, 1996
7	Jeff Lebo vs. Richmond, Nov. 28, 1987
7	Hubert Davis vs. Florida State, Dec. 15, 1991

MOST THREE–POINT FIELD GOALS MADE, SEASON

87   Kenny Smith, 1986–87
87   Donald Williams, 1994–95
85   Hubert Davis 1991–92
83   Donald Williams, 1992–93
78   Jeff Lebo, 1987–88

MOST THREE–POINT FIELD GOALS MADE, CAREER

221   Donald Williams, 1991-95
211   Jeff Lebo, 1985–89
197   Hubert Davis 1988–92
193   Dante Calabria, 1992-96
153   Rick Fox, 1987–91

MOST 3–POINT FIELD GOALS ATTEMPTED, GAME

14   Kenny Smith vs. SMU, Dec. 30, 1986
14   Jeff Lebo vs. Temple, Feb. 21, 1988
14   Jeff Lebo vs. Iowa, Jan. 7, 1989
14   Rick Fox vs. N.C. State, Feb. 6, 1991

MOST 3–POINT FIELD GOALS ATTEMPTED, SEASON

218   Donald Williams, 1994-95
213   Kenny Smith, 1986–87
199   Donald Williams, 1992–93
198   Hubert Davis, 1991–92
196   Rick Fox, 1990–91

MOST 3–POINT FIELD GOALS ATTEMPTED, CAREER

572   Donald Wiilliams, 1991-95
493   Jeff Lebo, 1985–89
469   Dante Calabria, 1992-96
453   Hubert Davis 1988–92
393   Rick Fox, 1987–91

HIGHEST 3–POINT FIELD GOAL PERCENTAGE, GAME

(Minimum five made)
1.000   Hubert Davis vs. Alabama, Nov. 30, 1989 (5 of 5 attempts); Hubert Davis vs. Eastern Michigan, March 22, 1991 (5 of 5 attempts)
.857   Jim Braddock vs. Rutgers, Jan. 5, 1983 (6 of 7 attempts); Michael Jordan vs. Georgia Tech, Jan. 29, 1983 (6 of 7 attempts); Dante Calabria vs. VMI, Dec.. 17, 1994 (6 of 7 attempts)

HIGHEST 3–POINT FIELD GOAL PERCENTAGE, SEASON

(Minimum 50 made)
.496   Dante Calabria, 1994-95 (66 of 133 attempts)
.489   Hubert Davis, 1990–91 (64 of 131 attempts)

HIGHEST 3–POINT FIELD GOAL PERCENTAGE, CAREER

(Minimum 100 made)
.435   Hubert Davis, 1988-92 (197 of 453 attempts)
.428   Jeff Lebo, 1985–89 (211 of 493 attempts)

MOST FREE THROWS MADE, GAME

21   York Larese vs. Duke, Dec. 29, 1959

MOST FREE THROWS MADE, SEASON

285   Lennie Rosenbluth, 1956–57
222   Bob Lewis, 1965–66
214   Pete Brennan, 1957–58
189   Lennie Rosenbluth, 1954–55
185   Pete Brennan, 1956–57
185   Jerry Stackhouse, 1994–95

MOST FREE THROWS MADE, CAREER

603   Lennie Rosenbluth, 1954–57
561   Sam Perkins, 1980–84
560   Phil Ford, 1974–78
512   Bob Lewis, 1964–67
506   Pete Brennan, 1955–58

MOST FREE THROWS ATTEMPTED, GAME

24   Lennie Rosenbluth vs. Clemson, Jan. 14, 1956; Billy Cunningham vs. Maryland, Jan. 13, 1964

MOST FREE THROWS ATTEMPTED, SEASON

376   Lennie Rosenbluth, 1956–57
291   Pete Brennan, 1957–58
274   Bob Lewis, 1965–66
262   Pete Brennan, 1956–57
260   Jerry Stackhouse, 1994-95

MOST FREE THROWS ATTEMPTED, CAREER

815   Lennie Rosenbluth, 1954–57
715   Pete Brennan, 1955–58
705   Sam Perkins, 1980–84
693   Phil Ford, 1974–78
661   Larry Miller, 1965–68

HIGHEST FREE THROW PERCENTAGE, GAME

(Minimum 15 made)
1.000   York Larese vs. Duke, Dec. 29, 1959 (21 of 21 attempts); Phil Ford vs. N.C. State, Feb. 24, 1976 (16 of 16 attempts)

HIGHEST FREE THROW PERCENTAGE, SEASON

(Minimum 75 made)
.878   Jeff Lebo, 1987–88 (86 of 98 attempts)
.876   Steve Hale, 1984–85 (85 of 97 attempts)
.871   Darrell Elston, 1973–74 (81 of 93 attempts)
.868   York Larese, 1959–60 (131 of 151 attempts)
.864   Jeff Lebo, 1988–89 (89 of 103 attempts)

HIGHEST FREE THROW PERCENTAGE, CAREER

(Minimum 100 made)
.839   Jeff Lebo, 1985–89 (308 of 367 attempts)
.835   Jim Braddock, 1979–83 (106 of 127 attempts)
.834   Dennis Wuycik, 1969–72 (431 of 517 attempts)
.833   Darrell Elston, 1971–74 (125 of 150 attempts)
.832   Ed Stahl, 1972–75 (124 of 149 attempts)

MOST REBOUNDS, GAME

30   Rusty Clark vs. Maryland, Feb. 21, 1968
28   Billy Cunningham vs. Maryland, Jan. 13, 1964
27   Billy Cunningham vs. Clemson, Feb. 16, 1963
25   Lennie Rosenbluth vs. S. Carolina, Dec. 9, 1954
25   Lennie Rosenbluth vs. Virginia, Jan. 11, 1955
25   Billy Cunningham vs. Tulane, Dec. 10, 1964

MOST REBOUNDS, SEASON

379   Billy Cunningham, 1963–64
365   George Lynch, 1992–93
349   Brad Daugherty, 1984–85
348   Bobby Jones, 1972–73
344   Billy Cunningham, 1964–65

MOST REBOUNDS, CAREER

1,167   Sam Perkins, 1980–84
1,097   George Lynch, 1989–93
1,062   Billy Cunningham, 1962–65
1,006   Mitch Kupchak, 1972–76
1,003   Brad Daugherty, 1982–86

HIGHEST REBOUNDING AVERAGE PER GAME, SEASON

16.1 Billy Cunningham, 1962–63 (339 rebounds in 21 games)
15.8 Billy Cunningham, 1963–64
14.3 Billy Cunningham, 1964–65
14.0 Doug Moe, 1960–61
11.7 Lennie Rosenbluth, 1954–55
11.7 Pete Brennan, 1957–58

HIGHEST REBOUNDING AVERAGE PER GAME, CAREER

15.4 Billy Cunningham, 1962–65 (1,062 rebounds in 69 games)
10.6 Doug Moe, 1958–61
10.5 Pete Brennan, 1955–58
10.4 Lennie Rosenbluth, 1954–57
10.2 Rusty Clark, 1966–69

MOST ASSISTS, GAME

17 Jeff Lebo vs. Tennessee–Chattanooga, Nov. 18, 1988
14 Phil Ford vs. Howard, Jan. 11, 1975
14 Phil Ford vs. Brigham Young, Dec. 20, 1976
14 Phil Ford vs. N.C. State, Feb. 23, 1977

MOST ASSISTS, SEASON

235 Kenny Smith, 1984–85
217 Phil Ford, 1976–77
217 King Rice, 1989–90
213 Jimmy Black, 1981–82
210 Kenny Smith, 1985–86

MOST ASSISTS, CAREER

768 Kenny Smith, 1983–87
753 Phil Ford, 1974–78
637 Derrick Phelps, 1990-94
629 King Rice, 1987–91
580 Jeff Lebo, 1985–89

HIGHEST ASSIST AVERAGE PER GAME, SEASON

7.0 Phil Ford, 1975–76
6.6 Phil Ford, 1976–77
6.5 Kenny Smith, 1984–85
6.4 King Rice, 1989–90
6.3 Jimmy Black, 1981–82
6.3 Derrick Phelps 1991–92

HIGHEST ASSIST AVERAGE PER GAME, CAREER

6.1 Phil Ford, 1974–78 (753 assists in 123 games)
6.1 Kenny Smith, 1983–87
5.2 Larry Brown, 1960–63
4.8 Derrick Phelps, 1990-94
4.6 Walter Davis, 1973–77

MOST STEALS, GAME

9 Derrick Phelps vs. Georgia Tech, Feb. 2, 1992
8 Derrick Phelps vs. Central Florida, Dec. 7, 1991
8 Dudley Bradley vs. Oregon State, Nov. 30, 1977
7 Dudley Bradley vs. Wake Forest, Dec. 1, 1978
7 Dudley Bradley vs. Duke, March 3, 1979
7 Jimmy Black vs. Tulsa, Dec. 3, 1981
7 Derrick Phelps vs. Houston, Dec. 13, 1992
7 Derrick Phelps vs. Cornell, Jan. 4, 1993
7 George Lynch vs. Florida State, Jan. 27, 1993
7 Derrick Phelps vs. Maryland, Feb. 10, 1994

MOST STEALS, SEASON

97 Dudley Bradley, 1978–79

MOST STEALS, CAREER

247 Derrick Phelps, 1990-94
241 George Lynch, 1989–93
197 Rick Fox, 1987–91
195 Kenny Smith, 1983–87

MOST BLOCKED SHOTS

Game — 9, Warren Martin vs. Stanford, Dec. 20, 1985
Season — 93, Rasheed Wallace, 1994-95
Career — 245, Sam Perkins, 1980–84

CAREER LEADERS

SCORING

Name (Years Played)	Points
1. Phil Ford (1974–78)	2,290
2. Sam Perkins (1980–84)	2,145
3. Lennie Rosenbluth (1954–57)	2,045
4. Al Wood (1977–81)	2,015
5. Charlie Scott (1967–70)	2,007
6. Larry Miller (1965–68)	1,982
7. Brad Daugherty (1982–86)	1,912
8. Walter Davis (1973–77)	1,863
9. Bob Lewis (1964–67)	1,836
10. Michael Jordan (1981–84)	1,788
11. Mike O'Koren (1976–80)	1,765
12. George Lynch (1989–93)	1,747
13. Billy Cunningham (1962–65)	1,709
14. Rick Fox (1987–91)	1,703
15. Kenny Smith (1983–87)	1,636
16. Eric Montross (1990–94)	1,627
17. Hubert Davis (1988–92)	1,615
18. Mitch Kupchak (1972–76)	1,611
19. Jeff Lebo (1985–89)	1,567
20. J.R. Reid (1986–89)	1,552

REBOUNDING

Name (Years Played)	Rebounds
1. Sam Perkins (1980–84)	1,167
2. George Lynch (1989–93)	1,097
3. Billy Cunningham (1962–65)	1,062
4. Mitch Kupchak (1972–76)	1,006
5. Brad Daugherty (1982–86)	1,003
6. Eric Montross (1990-94)	941
7. Rusty Clark (1966–69)	929
8. Scott Williams (1986–90)	861
9. Pete Brennan (1955–58)	854
10. Larry Miller (1965–68)	834
11. Bobby Jones (1971–74)	817
12. Mike O'Koren (1976–80)	815
13. Lennie Rosenbluth (1954–57)	790
14. Pete Chilcutt (1987–91)	766
15. J.R. Reid (1986–89)	731
16. Lee Dedmon (1968–71)	729
17. Joe Wolf (1983–87)	707
18. Jerry Vayda (1952–56)	687
19. Walter Davis (1973–77)	670
20. Bud Maddie (1950–54)	651

FIELD GOAL PERCENTAGE

(50.0 percent or better with at least 150 field goals made)

	Name (Years Played)	Made	Att.	Pct.
1.	Rasheed Wallace (1993–95)	377	594	.635
2.	Antawn Jamison (1995-)	201	322	.624
3.	Brad Daugherty (1982–86)	760	1,226	.620
4.	Bobby Jones (1971–74)	522	859	.608
5.	J.R. Reid (1986–89)	584	972	.601
6.	Warren Martin (1981–86)	256	431	.594
7.	Dennis Wuycik (1969–72)	519	880	.590
8.	Mitch Kupchak (1972–76)	651	1,110	.589
9.	Eric Montross (1990–94)	626	1,070	.585
10.	Tommy LaGarde (1973–77)	367	630	.583
11.	Kevin Madden (1985–90)	519	893	.581
12.	Sam Perkins (1980–84)	786	1,364	.576
13.	Mike O'Koren (1976–80)	643	1,124	.572
14.	Dave Chadwick (1968–71)	179	315	.568
15.	Curtis Hunter (1982–87)	201	357	.563
16.	Al Wood (1977–81)	825	1,474	.560
17.	John Virgil (1976–80)	233	419	.556
18.	Scott Williams (1986–90)	595	1,080	.551
19.	Joe Wolf (1983–87)	511	928	.551
20.	Charlie Shaffer (1961–64)	221	406	.544

FREE THROW PERCENTAGE

(70.0 percent or better with at least 100 free throws made)

	Name (Years Played)	Made	Att.	Pct.
1.	Jeff Lebo (1985–89)	308	367	.839
2.	Jim Braddock (1979–83)	106	127	.835
3.	Dennis Wuycik (1969–72)	431	517	.834
4.	Darrell Elston (1971–74)	125	150	.833
5.	Ed Stahl (1972–75)	124	149	.832
6.	Ranzino Smith (1984–88)	136	165	.824
7.	Kenny Smith (1983–87)	293	356	.823
8.	Hubert Davis (1989–92)	304	371	.819
9.	Steve Hale (1982–86)	230	283	.813
10.	Phil Ford (1974–78)	560	693	.808
11.	York Larese (1958–61)	351	441	.796
12.	Sam Perkins (1980–84)	561	705	.796
13.	Larry Brown (1960–63)	221	282	.784
14.	Tony Radovich (1952–56)	216	276	.783
15.	Ray Respess (1962–65)	110	141	.780
16.	George Karl (1970–73)	305	391	.780
17.	Bob Lewis (1964–67)	512	660	.776
18.	Pat Sullivan (1990–95)	120	155	.774
19.	Walter Davis (1973–77)	355	459	.773
20.	Lee Shaffer (1957–60)	253	330	.767

THREE–POINT FIELD GOAL PERCENTAGE

(40.0 percent or better with at least 25 three-point field goals made)

	Name (Years Played)	Made	Att.	Pct.
1.	Jim Braddock (1979–83)	43	93	.462
2.	Michael Jordan (1981–84)	34	76	.447
3.	Hubert Davis (1989–92)	197	453	.435
4.	Jeff Lebo (1985–89)	211	493	.428
5.	Steve Bucknall (1985–89)	71	168	.423
6.	Ranzino Smith (1984–88)	84	200	.420
7.	Jeff Denny (1986–90)	31	75	.413
8.	Dante Calabria (1992-96)	193	469	.412
9.	Kenny Smith (1983–87)	87	213	.408

ASSISTS

	Name (Years Played)	Assists
1.	Kenny Smith (1983–87)	768
2.	Phil Ford (1974–78)	753
3.	Derrick Phelps (1990–94)	637
4.	King Rice (1987–91)	629
5.	Jeff Lebo (1985–89)	580
6.	Jimmy Black (1978–82)	525
7.	Steve Hale (1982–86)	503
8.	Matt Doherty (1980–84)	446
9.	Jeff McInnis (1993-96)	435
10.	Walter Davis (1973–77)	409
11.	George Karl (1970–73)	394
12.	Steve Bucknall (1985–89)	382
13.	John Kuester (1973–77)	370
14.	Mike O'Koren (1976–80)	348
15.	Dante Calabria (1992-96)	336
16.	Rick Fox (1987–91)	323
17.	Charlie Scott (1967–70)	310
18.	Larry Miller (1965–68)	309
19.	Henrik Rödl (1989–93)	303
20.	Dick Grubar (1966–69)	296

STEALS

	Name (Years Played)	Steals
1.	Derrick Phelps (1990–94)	247
2.	George Lynch (1989–93)	241
3.	Rick Fox (1987–91)	197
4.	Kenny Smith (1983–87)	195
5.	Dudley Bradley (1975–79)	190
6.	Mike O'Koren (1976–80)	183
7.	Jimmy Black (1978–82)	175
8.	Michael Jordan (1981–84)	169
9.	Steve Hale (1982–86)	164
10.	Phil Ford (1974–78)	163

BLOCKED SHOTS

	Name (Years Played)	Blocks
1.	Sam Perkins (1980–84)	245
2.	Warren Martin (1981–86)	190
3.	Kevin Salvadori (1990–94)	174
4.	Eric Montross (1990–94)	169
5.	Scott Williams (1986–90)	161
6.	Rasheed Wallace (1993–95)	156
7.	Brad Daugherty (1982–86)	146
8.	James Worthy (1979–82)	94
9.	J.R. Reid (1986–89)	86
10.	Pete Chilcutt (1987–91)	83

YEARLY LEADERS

FIELD GOAL PERCENTAGE

(At least 85 field goals made)

Year	Player	FGM	FGA	PCT
1951–52	Al Lifson	163	401	.406
1952–53	Jerry Vayda	111	266	.417
1953–54	Jerry Vayda	123	298	.413
1954–55	Tony Radovich	85	194	.438
1955–56	Lennie Rosenbluth	227	496	.456
1956–57	Lennie Rosenbluth	305	631	.483
1957–58	Pete Brennan	170	388	.438
1958–59	Lee Shaffer	128	273	.468
1959–60	Lee Shaffer	169	388	.436
1960–61	Jim Hudock	94	188	.500
1961–62	Donnie Walsh	85	152	.559
1962–63	Billy Cunningham	186	380	.487
1963–64	Charlie Shaffer	117	221	.525
1964–65	Billy Cunningham	237	481	.491
1965–66	Larry Miller	219	400	.548
1966–67	Rusty Clark	181	328	.552
1967–68	Charlie Scott	234	470	.498
1968–69	Bill Bunting	217	363	.598
1969–70	Dennis Wuycik	148	270	.548
1970–71	Dennis Wuycik	182	300	.607
1971–72	Bobby Jones	127	190	.668
1972–73	Mitch Kupchak	99	164	.604
1973–74	Bobby Jones	189	326	.580
1974–75	Mitch Kupchak	239	397	.602
1975–76	Tommy LaGarde	156	255	.612
1976–77	Tommy LaGarde	108	182	.593
1977–78	Mike O'Koren	173	269	.643
1978–79	Al Wood	210	367	.572
1979–80	Al Wood	216	378	.571
1980–81	Sam Perkins	199	318	.626
1981–82	Sam Perkins	174	301	.578
1982–83	Brad Daugherty	110	197	.558
1983–84	Brad Daugherty	128	210	.610
1984–85	Brad Daugherty	238	381	.625
1985–86	Brad Daugherty	284	438	.648
1986–87	J.R. Reid	198	339	.584
1987–88	J.R. Reid	222	366	.607
1988–89	J.R. Reid	164	267	.614
1989–90	Kevin Madden	120	211	.569
1990–91	Pete Chilcutt	175	325	.538
1991–92	Eric Montross	140	244	.574
1992–93	Eric Montross	222	361	.615
1993–94	Rasheed Wallace	139	230	.604
1994–95	Rasheed Wallace	238	364	.654
1995–96	Antawn Jamison	201	322	.624

FREE THROW PERCENTAGE

(At least 50 free throws made)

Year	Player	FTM	FTA	PCT
1951–52	Al Lifson	99	140	.707
1952–53	Al Lifson	100	142	.704
1953–54	Al Lifson	74	97	.763
1954–55	Tony Radovich	60	80	.750
1955–56	Tony Radovich	63	76	.829
1956–57	Lennie Rosenbluth	285	376	.758
1957–58	Harvey Salz	64	84	.761
1958–59	Lee Shaffer	74	96	.770
1959–60	York Larese	131	151	.868
1960–61	York Larese	124	158	.785
1961–62	Larry Brown	101	127	.795
1962–63	Larry Brown	95	122	.779
1963–64	Ray Respess	52	66	.788
1964–65	Bob Lewis	123	175	.703
1965–66	Bob Lewis	222	274	.810
1966–67	Bob Lewis	167	211	.791

Year	Player	FGM	FGA	PCT
1967–68	Dick Grubar	64	90	.711
1968–69	Bill Bunting	143	173	.827
1969–70	Charlie Scott	169	215	.786
1970–71	Dennis Wuycik	169	197	.858
1971–72	Kim Huband	53	57	.930
1972–73	Ed Stahl	73	88	.830
1973–74	Darrell Elston	81	93	.871
1974–75	Phil Ford	126	161	.783
1975–76	Tommy LaGarde	106	131	.809
1976–77	Phil Ford	157	184	.853
1977–78	Phil Ford	149	184	.810
1978–79	Mike O'Koren	144	188	.766
1979–80	Al Wood	118	154	.766
1980–81	Jimmy Black	93	118	.788
1981–82	Matt Doherty	71	92	.772
1982–83	Jim Braddock	67	81	.827
1983–84	Sam Perkins	155	181	.856
1984–85	Steve Hale	85	97	.876
1985–86	Steve Hale	85	103	.825
1986–87	Jeff Lebo	79	93	.849
1987–88	Ranzino Smith	52	58	.897
1988–89	Jeff Lebo	89	103	.864
1989–90	Hubert Davis	59	74	.797
1990–91	Hubert Davis	81	97	.835
1991–92	Hubert Davis	140	169	.828
1992–93	Donald Williams	97	117	.829
1993–94	Donald Williams	77	100	.770
1994–95	Jerry Stackhouse	185	260	.712
1995–96	Jeff McInnis	88	110	.800

THREE–POINT FIELD GOAL PERCENTAGE

(At least 25 three–point field goals made)

Year	Player	FGM	FGA	PCT
1982–83	Jim Braddock	43	93	.462
1986–87	Jeff Lebo	67	149	.450
1987–88	Jeff Lebo	78	168	.464
1988–89	Steve Bucknall	62	148	.419
1989–90	Rick Fox	70	160	.438
1990–91	Hubert Davis	64	131	.489
1991–92	Hubert Davis	85	198	.429
1992–93	Donald Williams	83	199	.417
1993–94	Jeff McInnis	27	65	.415
1994–95	Dante Calabria	66	133	.496
1995–96	Shammond Williams	46	116	.397

SCORING AVERAGE

Year	Player	PPG
1951–52	Al Lifson	15.8
1952–53	Al Lifson	14.7
1953–54	Jerry Vayda	17.0
1954–55	Lennie Rosenbluth	25.5
1955–56	Lennie Rosenbluth	26.7
1956–57	Lennie Rosenbluth	28.0
1957–58	Pete Brennan	21.3
1958–59	York Larese	15.1
1959–60	Lee Shaffer	18.2
1960–61	York Larese	23.1
1961–62	Larry Brown	16.5
1962–63	Billy Cunningham	22.7
1963–64	Billy Cunningham	26.0
1964–65	Billy Cunningham	25.4
1965–66	Bob Lewis	27.4
1966–67	Larry Miller	21.9
1967–68	Larry Miller	22.4
1968–69	Charlie Scott	22.3
1969–70	Charlie Scott	27.1
1970–71	Dennis Wuycik	18.4
1971–72	Robert McAdoo	19.5
1972–73	George Karl	17.0

1973–74	Bobby Jones	16.1
1974–75	Mitch Kupchak	18.5
1975–76	Phil Ford	18.6
1976–77	Phil Ford	18.7
1977–78	Phil Ford	20.8
1978–79	Al Wood	17.8
1979–80	Al Wood	19.0
1980–81	Al Wood	18.1
1981–82	James Worthy	15.6
1982–83	Michael Jordan	20.0
1983–84	Michael Jordan	19.6
1984–85	Brad Daugherty	17.3
1985–86	Brad Daugherty	20.2
1986–87	Kenny Smith	16.9
1987–88	J.R. Reid	18.0
1988–89	J.R. Reid	15.9
1989–90	Rick Fox	16.2
1990–91	Rick Fox	16.9
1991–92	Hubert Davis	21.4
1992–93	Eric Montross	15.8
1993–94	Donald Williams	14.3
1994–95	Jerry Stackhouse	19.2
1995–96	Jeff McInnis	16.5

REBOUNDING AVERAGE

Year	Player	RPG
1951–52	Howard Deasy	10.7
1952–53	Bud Maddie	11.6
1953–54	Paul Likins	10.9
1954–55	Lennie Rosenbluth	11.7
1955–56	Lennie Rosenbluth	11.5
1956–57	Pete Brennan	10.4
1957–58	Pete Brennan	11.7
1958–59	Dick Kepley	7.3
1959–60	Doug Moe	11.3
1960–61	Doug Moe	14.0
1961–62	Jim Hudock	10.1
1962–63	Billy Cunningham	16.1
1963–64	Billy Cunningham	15.8
1964–65	Billy Cunningham	14.3
1965–66	Larry Miller	10.3
1966–67	Rusty Clark	10.3
1967–68	Rusty Clark	11.0
1968–69	Rusty Clark	9.2
1969–70	Lee Dedmon	9.4
1970–71	Lee Dedmon	8.5
1971–72	Robert McAdoo	10.1
1972–73	Bobby Jones	10.5
1973–74	Bobby Jones	9.8
1974–75	Mitch Kupchak	10.8
1975–76	Mitch Kupchak	11.3
1976–77	Tommy LaGarde	7.4
1977–78	Mike O'Koren	6.7
1978–79	Mike O'Koren	7.2
1979–80	Mike O'Koren	7.4
1980–81	James Worthy	8.4
1981–82	Sam Perkins	7.8
1982–83	Sam Perkins	9.4
1983–84	Sam Perkins	9.6
1984–85	Brad Daugherty	9.7
1985–86	Brad Daugherty	9.0
1986–87	J.R. Reid	7.4
1987–88	J.R. Reid	8.9
1988–89	Scott Williams	7.3
1989–90	Scott Williams	7.3
1990–91	George Lynch	7.4
1991–92	George Lynch	8.8
1992–93	George Lynch	9.6
1993–94	Eric Montross	8.1
1994–95	Jerry Stackhouse	8.2
1995–96	Antawn Jamison	9.7

BLOCKED SHOTS

Year	Player	Total Blocks
1975–76	Mitch Kupchak	32
1976–77	Tommy LaGarde	31
1977–78	Jeff Wolf	23
1978–79	Pete Budko	27
1979–80	Jeff Wolf	28
1980–81	Sam Perkins	67
1981–82	Sam Perkins	53
1982–83	Sam Perkins	65
1983–84	Sam Perkins	60
1984–85	Warren Martin	81
1985–86	Warren Martin	81
1986–87	David Popson	27
	J.R. Reid	27
	Scott Williams	27
1987–88	Scott Williams	43
1988–89	Scott Williams	50
1989–90	Scott Williams	41
1990–91	Pete Chilcutt	35
1991–92	Kevin Salvadori	63
1992–93	Eric Montross	47
1993–94	Rasheed Wallace	63
1994–95	Rasheed Wallace	93
1995–96	Serge Zwikker	49

ASSISTS

Year	Player	Total Assists
1968–69	Charlie Scott	108
1969–70	Eddie Fogler	92
1970–71	Steve Previs	90
1971–72	Steve Previs	151
1972–73	George Karl	192
1973–74	Darrell Elston	158
1974–75	Phil Ford	161
1975–76	Phil Ford	203
1976–77	Phil Ford	217
1977–78	Phil Ford	172
1978–79	Mike O'Koren	99
1979–80	Mike O'Koren	104
1980–81	Jimmy Black	188
1981–82	Jimmy Black	213
1982–83	Matt Doherty	150
1983–84	Matt Doherty	124
1984–85	Kenny Smith	235
1985–86	Kenny Smith	210
1986–87	Kenny Smith	209
1987–88	Jeff Lebo	159
1988–89	Steve Bucknall	196
1989–90	King Rice	217
1990–91	King Rice	207
1991–92	Derrick Phelps	207
1992–93	Derrick Phelps	196
1993–94	Derrick Phelps	176
1994–95	Jeff McInnis	180
1995–96	Jeff McInnis	170

STEALS

Year	Player	Total Steals
1975–76	Walter Davis	71
1976–77	Walter Davis	78
1977–78	Dudley Bradley	61
1978–79	Dudley Bradley	97
1979–80	Mike O'Koren	43
1980–81	Jimmy Black	64
1981–82	Jimmy Black	58
1982–83	Michael Jordan	78
1983–84	Michael Jordan	50
1984–85	Kenny Smith	64
1985–86	Steve Hale	55
1986–87	Kenny Smith	51

1987–88	Scott Williams	45
1988–89	Rick Fox	47
1989–90	Rick Fox	54
	King Rice	54
1990–91	Rick Fox	70
1991–92	Derrick Phelps	78
1992–93	George Lynch	89
1993–94	Derrick Phelps	60
1994–95	Jerry Stackhouse	50
1995–96	Jeff McInnis	38

HONORS

NATIONAL PLAYERS OF THE YEAR

Jack Cobb: Helms Foundation, 1926
George Glamack: Helms Foundation, 1940, 1941
Lennie Rosenbluth: Helms Foundation, 1957
Phil Ford: U.S. Basketball Writers Association, National Association of Basketball Coaches, The Sporting News, John Wooden Award, 1978
James Worthy: Helms Foundation, 1982 (Co–Winner)
Michael Jordan: The Sporting News, 1983; The Sporting News, Associated Press, United Press International, U.S. Basketball Writers Association, National Association of Basketball Coaches, Basketball Weekly, John Wooden Award, Naismith Award, 1984
Kenny Smith: Basketball Times, 1987
Jerry Stackhouse: Sports Illustrated, 1995

ALL–AMERICANS

(All First–Team Selections Unless Otherwise Noted)
Cartwright Carmichael: 1923, 1924
Jack Cobb: 1924, 1925, 1926
George Glamack: 1940, 1941
Jim Jordan: Helms Foundation, 1945 (2nd Team)
John "Hook" Dillon: The Sporting News, 1946; Maxwell, 1946; Converse,1946
Lennie Rosenbluth: Associated Press, 1956 (2nd Team), 1957; United Press International, 1956 (2nd Team), 1957; Helms Foundation, 1956, 1957; NEA, 1956 (3rd Team), 1957; Colliers, 1956 (3rd Team), 1957; Converse, 1956 (2nd Team), 1957; USBWA, 1957
Tommy Kearns: Converse, 1957 (2nd Team); Associated Press, 1958 (3rd Team)
Pete Brennan: Associated Press, 1958; The Sporting News, 1958; USBWA, 1958; Converse, 1958; United Press International, 1958 (2nd Team), Helms Foundation, 1958 (2nd Team)
Lee Shaffer: American Weekly, 1959 (3rd Team); USBWA, 1960
York Larese: Associated Press, 1959 (3rd Team); Coaches, 1960 (3rd Team), 1961 (2nd Team); The Sporting News, 1961 (2nd Team); NEA, 1961 (2nd Team); United Press International, 1961 (3rd Team); Converse, 1961 (2nd Team)
Doug Moe: The Sporting News, 1959 (2nd Team); USBWA, 1961, The Sporting News, 1961 (2nd Team)
Billy Cunningham: USBWA, 1964, 1965; Helms Foundation, 1965; The Sporting News, 1965 (2nd Team)
Bob Lewis: Helms Foundation, 1966, 1967; Associated Press, 1966 (2nd Team)
Larry Miller: USBWA, 1967, 1968; Helms Foundation, 1967, 1968; Converse, 1967, 1968; Associated Press, 1968; United Press International, 1968; Coaches, 1968

Charlie Scott: USBWA, 1969, 1970; Coaches, 1969, 1970; Helms Foundation, 1969, 1970; Converse, 1969, 1970; Basketball Weekly, 1969, 1970; NBA Coaches, 1970; Associated Press, 1970 (2nd Team); United Press International, 1970 (2nd Team); NEA, 1970
Bill Chamberlain: NBA Coaches, 1972 (2nd Team)
Robert McAdoo: NBA Coaches, 1972; Helms Foundation, 1972; NEA, 1972; The Sporting News, 1972; Associated Press, 1972 (2nd Team)
Dennis Wuycik: Helms Foundation, 1972; Basketball Weekly, 1972
Bobby Jones: USBWA, 1974; Coaches, 1974 (2nd Team); Associated Press, 1974 (2nd Team); United Press International, 1974 (2nd Team)
Mitch Kupchak: Citizen Savings (Helms Foundation), 1975, 1976; USBWA, 1976; Coaches, 1976; Converse, 1976; Associated Press, 1976 (2nd Team); United Press International, 1976 (2nd Team); Basketball Weekly, 1976 (3rd Team)
Phil Ford: Basketball Weekly, 1976, 1977, 1978; Coaches, 1976, 1977, 1978; Associated Press, 1976 (2nd Team), 1977, 1978; United Press International, 1976 (2nd Team), 1977 (2nd Team), 1978; Citizen Savings (Helms Foundation), 1976, 1977, 1978; Sporting News, 1976, 1977 (2nd Team), 1978; USBWA, 1977, 1978
Tommy LaGarde: The Sporting News, 1977 (2nd Team)
Mike O'Koren: Citizen Savings (Helms Foundation), 1978, 1979, 1980; Converse, 1978, 1979, 1980; Basketball Weekly, 1978 (2nd Team), 1979, 1980 (2nd Team); USBWA, 1979, 1980; The Sporting News, 1979, 1980; Coaches, 1979 (2nd Team), 1980 (2nd Team); United Press International, 1979 (2nd Team), 1980 (3rd Team)
Al Wood: Converse, 1980, 1981; USBWA, 1981; Citizen Savings (Helms Foundation), 1981; Associated Press, 1981 (2nd Team); NABC, 1981 (2nd Team)
James Worthy: USBWA, 1981, 1982; United Press International, 1982; NABC, 1982; The Sporting News, 1982; Basketball Weekly, 1982; Naismith, 1982; NBA Coaches, 1982; Converse, 1982; First Interstate Bank (Helms Foundation), 1982; Associated Press, 1982 (2nd Team)
Sam Perkins: USBWA, 1982, 1983, 1984; Converse, 1982, 1983, 1984; First Interstate Bank (Helms Foundation), 1982, 1983, 1984; United Press International, 1982 (2nd Team), 1983, 1984; Naismith, 1982 (2nd Team), 1983, 1984; The Sporting News, 1982 (2nd Team), 1983 (2nd Team), 1984; Basketball Weekly, 1982 (2nd Team), 1983 (2nd Team), 1984; NABC, 1982 (2nd Team), 1983 (2nd Team), 1984 (2nd Team); ESPN, 1983, 1984; ABAUSA, 1983, 1984; Associated Press, 1983 (3rd Team), 1984; Basketball Times, 1983 (3rd Team), 1984; NBA Coaches, 1984
Michael Jordan: Associated Press, 1983, 1984; United Press International, 1983, 1984; The Sporting News, 1983, 1984; USBWA, 1983, 1984; NABC, 1983, 1984; Naismith, 1983, 1984; NBA Coaches, 1983, 1984; Basketball Weekly, 1983, 1984; ESPN, 1983, 1984; ABAUSA, 1983, 1984; Basketball Times, 1983, 1984; First Interstate Bank (Helms Foundation), 1983, 1984; Converse, 1983, 1984

Brad Daugherty: USBWA, 1986; Basketball Weekly, 1986; Associated Press, 1986 (2nd Team); United Press International, 1986 (2nd Team); NABC, 1986 (2nd Team); The Sporting News, 1986 (2nd Team)

Kenny Smith: Associated Press, 1987; United Press International, 1987; USBWA, 1987; NABC, 1987; Basketball Times, 1987; Basketball Weekly, 1987; The Sporting News, 1987; Naismith Board, 1987; First Interstate Bank (Helms Foundation), 1987; Converse, 1987

J.R. Reid: Associated Press, 1988; Basketball Weekly, 1988; USBWA, 1988; United Press International, 1988 (2nd Team); The Sporting News, 1988 (2nd Team); Basketball Times, 1988, 1989 (3rd Team); NABC, 1988, 1989 (3rd Team)

Rick Fox: The Sporting News, 1991 (3rd Team)

Eric Montross: Naismith, 1994; Classic Games John R. Wooden All–America Team, 1993, 1994; Associated Press, 1993 (2nd Team), 1994 (2nd Team); NABC, 1993 (2nd Team), 1994; The Sporting News, 1993 (2nd Team), 1994 (2nd Team); Basketball Weekly, 1993 (2nd Team), 1994; United Press International, 1993 (3rd Team); Basketball Times, 1993 (3rd Team), 1994; USBWA, 1994 (Honorable Mention)

George Lynch: United Press International, 1993 (Honorable Mention)

Derrick Phelps: Associated Press, 1994 (Honorable Mention)

Jerry Stackhouse: Associated Press, 1995; United Press International, 1995; USBWA, 1995; NABC, 1995; John Wooden Team, 1995; The Sporting News, 1995 (2nd Team); Basketball Times, 1995 (2nd Team)

Rasheed Wallace: The Sporting News, 1995; Basketball Times, 1995; John Wooden Team, 1995; Associated Press, 1995 (2nd Team); United Press International, 1995 (2nd Team); USBWA, 1995 (2nd Team); NABC, 1995 (2nd Team)

Antawn Jamison: Basketball Weekly, 1996 (Honorable Mention)

NAISMITH MEMORIAL BASKETBALL HALL OF FAME

Frank J. McGuire: Coach
Dean Smith: Coach
Billy Cunningham: Player
Bernard Carnevale: Coach

NATIONAL COACHES OF THE YEAR

Frank McGuire: United Press International, 1957
Dean Smith: National Association of Basketball Coaches, 1977; U.S. Basketball Writers Association, Basketball Weekly, 1979; Medalist, 1982; Naismith, 1993

ATLANTIC COAST CONFERENCE PLAYERS OF THE YEAR

Lennie Rosenbluth: 1957
Pete Brennan: 1958
Lee Shaffer: 1960
Billy Cunningham: 1965
Larry Miller: 1967, 1968
Mitch Kupchak: 1976
Phil Ford: 1978
Michael Jordan: 1984

ACC COACHES OF THE YEAR

Frank McGuire: 1957
Dean Smith: 1967, 1968, 1971, 1976, 1977, 1979, 1988, 1993

USBWA DISTRICT COACH OF THE YEAR

Dean Smith: 1993

JOE LAPCHICK TROPHY

(Top senior college basketball player)
Sam Perkins: 1984

MEMBERS OF ALL–SOUTHERN CONFERENCE TEAMS

Cartwright Carmichael: 1922, 1923, 1924
Monk McDonald: 1922, 1924
Jack Cobb: 1924, 1925, 1926
Bill Dodderer: 1924, 1925, 1926
Artie Newcombe: 1926
Tom Alexander: 1932
Virgil Weathers: 1932
Jim McCachren: 1934, 1935, 1936
Stewart "Snooks" Aitken: 1935
Ivan "Jack" Glace: 1935
Earl Ruth: 1937
Paul Severin: 1940
George Glamack: 1940, 1941
Bob Rose: 1941, 1942
Boyce Box: 1944
Bernie Mock: 1944
Manny Alvarez: 1945
Jim Jordan: 1945
John "Hook" Dillon: 1946
Jim White: 1947
Bob Paxton: 1947, 1948
Coy Carson: 1949
Hugo Kappler: 1949

ALL–SOUTHERN CONFERENCE TOURNAMENT TEAMS

(All First–Team Selections Unless Otherwise Noted)
Cartwright Carmichael: 1924
Monk McDonald: 1924
Jack Cobb: 1925, 1926
Bunn Hackney: 1926, 1927 (2nd Team)
Artie Newcombe: 1926
Bill Dodderer: 1926 (2nd Team)
John Purser: 1927 (2nd Team)
Tom Alexander: 1932
Virgil Weathers: 1932, 1933 (2nd Team), 1934
Wilmer Hines: 1932 (2nd Team), 1933 (2nd Team)
Stewart "Snooks" Aitken: 1934, 1935
Ivan "Jack" Glace: 1934, 1935
Jim McCachren: 1934, 1935, 1936
Melvin Nelson: 1935 (2nd Team)
Andy Bershak: 1936 (2nd Team), 1937 (2nd Team)
Earl Ruth: 1936 (2nd Team), 1937, 1938 (2nd Team)
Ramsay Potts: 1937 (2nd Team)
George Glamack: 1940, 1941 (2nd Team)
Jimmy Howard: 1940 (2nd Team)
Bob Rose: 1941
Bernie Mock: 1944
Boyce Box: 1944
John Dewell: 1944 (2nd Team)
Jack Fitch: 1944 (2nd Team)
Manny Alvarez: 1945
Jim Jordan: 1945, 1946 (2nd Team)
John "Hook" Dillon: 1945 (2nd Team), 1946 (2nd Team)
Bob Paxton: 1945 (2nd Team), 1947, 1948
Horace "Bones" McKinney: 1946 (2nd Team)
Jim White: 1947
Jim Hamilton: 1947 (2nd Team)

ALL–ATLANTIC COAST CONFERENCE TEAMS

(All First–Team Selections Unless Otherwise Noted)
Jerry Vayda: 1954 (2nd Team)
Lennie Rosenbluth: 1955, 1956, 1957
Tommy Kearns: 1957, 1958

Pete Brennan: 1957 (2nd Team), 1958
Doug Moe: 1959, 1961
Lee Shaffer: 1959 (2nd Team), 1960
York Larese: 1959, 1960, 1961
Larry Brown: 1962 (2nd Team), 1963
Jim Hudock: 1962 (2nd Team)
Billy Cunningham: 1963, 1964, 1965
Bob Lewis: 1965 (2nd Team), 1966, 1967
Larry Miller: 1966 (2nd Team), 1967, 1968
Rusty Clark: 1968 (2nd Team)
Charlie Scott: 1968, 1969, 1970
Bill Bunting: 1969
Dick Grubar: 1969 (2nd Team)
Dennis Wuycik: 1971, 1972
George Karl: 1971 (2nd Team), 1972 (2nd Team), 1973
Robert McAdoo: 1972
Bill Chamberlain: 1972 (2nd Team)
Bobby Jones: 1973 (2nd Team), 1974
Darrell Elston: 1974 (2nd Team)
Mitch Kupchak: 1975, 1976
Walter Davis: 1976 (2nd Team), 1977
Phil Ford: 1976, 1977, 1978
Tommy LaGarde: 1977 (2nd Team)
Mike O'Koren: 1978, 1979 (2nd Team), 1980
Al Wood: 1979, 1980 (2nd Team), 1981
James Worthy: 1981 (2nd Team), 1982
Sam Perkins: 1982, 1983, 1984
Michael Jordan: 1983, 1984
Brad Daugherty: 1985, 1986

Kenny Smith: 1985 (2nd Team), 1986 (2nd Team), 1987
Steve Hale: 1986 (2nd Team)
Joe Wolf: 1987
J.R. Reid: 1987 (2nd Team), 1988
Jeff Lebo: 1988 (2nd Team)
Steve Bucknall: 1989 (2nd Team)
Kevin Madden: 1989 (2nd Team)
Rick Fox: 1990 (3rd Team), 1991
Pete Chilcutt: 1991 (3rd Team)
Hubert Davis: 1992 (2nd Team)
George Lynch: 1992 (3rd Team), 1993
Eric Montross: 1993, 1994 (2nd Team)
Derrick Phelps: 1993 (Honorable Mention), 1994 (2nd Team)
Brian Reese: 1993 (Honorable Mention), 1994 (Honorable Mention)
Donald Williams: 1993 (Honorable Mention), 1994 (Honorable Mention), 1995 (Honorable Mention)
Rasheed Wallace: 1994 (Honorable Mention), 1995
Jerry Stackhouse: 1994 (Honorable Mention), 1995
Kevin Salvadori: 1994 (Honorable Mention)
Dante Calabria: 1995 (Honorable Mention); 1996 (3rd Team)
Jeff McInnis: 1995 (3rd Team), 1996 (2nd Team)
Antawn Jamison: 1996

TAR HEELS IN THE NBA DRAFT

Year	Player	NBA Team	Round	# Pick	Overall
1948	Norman Kohler	Indianapolis Olympians	n/a	n/a	n/a
1948	Bob Paxton	Indianapolis Olympians	n/a	n/a	n/a
1957	Len Rosenbluth	Philadelphia Warriors	1st	6	6
1958	Pete Brennan	New York Knicks	1st	4	4
1958	Joe Quigg	New York Knicks	2nd	4	12
1958	Tommy Kearns	Syracuse Nationals	4th	6	29
1960	Lee Shaffer	Syracuse Nationals	1st	5	5
1960	Doug Moe	Detroit Pistons	7th	4	52
1961	York Larese	Chicago Packers	2nd	11	20
1961	Doug Moe	Chicago Packers	2nd	13	22
1961	Dick Kepley	St. Louis Hawks	11th	7	98
1962	Jim Hudock	Philadelphia Warriors	6th	7	50
1962	Ken McComb	Philadelphia Warriors	10th	6	84
1962	Donnie Walsh	Philadelphia Warriors	11th	5	89
1963	Larry Brown	Baltimore Bullets	7th	2	55
1965	Billy Cunningham	Philadelphia 76ers	1st	4	4
1966	Bob Bennett	New York Knicks	13th	1	101
1967	Bob Lewis	San Francisco Warriors	4th	8	39
1967	Mark Mirken	New York Knicks	11th	4	117
1968	Larry Miller	Philadelphia 76ers	5th	12	62
1969	Bill Bunting	New York Knicks	2nd	11	26
1969	Dick Grubar	Los Angeles Lakers	6th	12	83
1969	Rusty Clark	Detroit Pistons	11th	4	145
1970	Charlie Scott	Boston Celtics	7th	4	106
1971	Lee Dedmon	Los Angeles Lakers	5th	13	81
1972	Bob McAdoo	Buffalo Braves	1st	2	2
1972	Dennis Wuycik	Boston Celtics	2nd	14	27
1972	Bill Chamberlain	Golden State Warriors	3rd	13	43
1972	Steve Previs	Boston Celtics	7th	14	111
1973	George Karl	New York Knicks	4th	14	66
1973	Donn Johnston	Buffalo Braves	18th	1	207
1974	Bobby Jones	Houston Rockets	1st	5	5
1974	Darrell Elston	Atlanta Hawks	3rd	7	43
1974	John O'Donnell	New York Knicks	10th	14	174
1975	Donald Washington	New York Knicks	5th	8	80
1975	Ed Stahl	Kansas City-Omaha Kings	5th	13	85

1976	Mitch Kupchak	Washington Bullets	1st	13	13
1977	Walter Davis	Phoenix Suns	1st	5	5
1977	Tommy LaGarde	Denver Nuggets	1st	9	9
1977	John Kuester	Kansas City Kings	3rd	9	53
1977	Bruce Buckley	San Antonio Spurs	6th	15	125
1978	Phil Ford	Kansas City Kings	1st	2	2
1978	Geff Crompton	Kansas City Kings	4th	4	70
1978	Tom Zaliagiris	Milwaukee Bucks	8th	12	164
1979	Dudley Bradley	Indiana Pacers	1st	13	13
1980	Mike O'Koren	New Jersey Nets	1st	6	6
1980	John Virgil	Golden State Warriors	3rd	3	49
1980	Rich Yonakor	San Antonio Spurs	3rd	15	61
1980	Jeff Wolf	Milwaukee Bucks	4th	17	86
1980	Dave Colescott	Utah Jazz	7th	2	140
1981	Al Wood	Atlanta Hawks	1st	4	4
1981	Pete Budko	Dallas Mavericks	5th	1	93
1981	Mike Pepper	San Diego Clippers	6th	8	123
1982	James Worthy	Los Angeles Lakers	1st	1	1
1982	Jimmy Black	New Jersey Nets	3rd	13	59
1982	Chris Brust	Denver Nuggets	6th	16	131
1982	Jeb Barlow	Denver Nuggets	7th	15	153
1983	Jimmy Braddock	Denver Nuggets	5th	14	107
1984	Michael Jordan	Chicago Bulls	1st	3	3
1984	Sam Perkins	Dallas Mavericks	1st	4	4
1984	Matt Doherty	Cleveland Cavaliers	6th	8	119
1984	Cecil Exum	Denver Nuggets	9th	10	194
1985	Buzz Peterson	Cleveland Cavaliers	7th	8	147
1986	Brad Daugherty	Cleveland Cavaliers	1st	1	1
1986	Warren Martin	Cleveland Cavaliers	4th	3	73
1986	Steve Hale	New Jersey Nets	4th	11	81
1987	Kenny Smith	Sacramento Kings	1st	6	6
1987	Joe Wolf	Los Angeles Clippers	1st	13	13
1987	Dave Popson	Detroit Pistons	4th	19	88
1987	Curtis Hunter	Denver Nuggets	7th	18	156
1989	J.R. Reid	Charlotte Hornets	1st	5	5
1991	Rick Fox	Boston Celtics	1st	24	24
1991	Pete Chilcutt	Sacramento Kings	1st	27	27
1992	Hubert Davis	New York Knicks	1st	20	20
1993	George Lynch	Los Angeles Lakers	1st	12	12
1994	Eric Montross	Boston Celtics	1st	9	9
1995	Jerry Stackhouse	Philadelphia 76ers	1st	3	3
1995	Rasheed Wallace	Washington Bullets	1st	4	4
1996	Jeff McInnis	Denver Nuggets	2nd	8	37

79 Carolina players drafted by NBA teams, 27 first-round picks

ALL-TIME LETTERMEN

A Aiken, Ben 1939-41 (M); Aitken, Stewart "Snooks" 1933-1935; Alexander, Tom 1930-32; Allen, Bill 1945; Altemose, Bob 1943-44; Alvarez, Manny 1945; Anderson, Don 1944-46; Andrews, Ezra 1914-16; Austin, John 1971.

B Baines, Greg 1990-92 (M); Baldwin, Janet 1986-87 (M); Barber, Howard 1925; Barlow, Jeb 1981-82; Barner, Maria 1996 (M); Barnes, Octavus 1995; Barrett, Jon 1971-72; Bartel, Heidi 1996 (M); Beale, William 1933-34; Bell, Mickey 1973-75; Bennett, Andy 1936-38; Black, Jimmy 1979-82; Blizzard, Rolf 1994-95 (M); Blood, Ernest 1934-35; Bloxam, Eran 1992-94 (M); Bondshu, Bill 1994-95 (M); Boone, Pete 1938; Bostick, Jim 1967; Bowers, Bruce 1962; Bowman, Dave 1940; Box, Boyce 1944; Braddock, Jim 1980-83; Bradley, Dudley 1976-79; Brandt, George 1932-33; Branson, Les 1939; Breen, Samuel 1932 (M); Brennan, Pete 1956-58; Brown, Bill 1963-65; Brown, Joe 1967-69; Brown, Larry 1961-63; Brown, Lou 1959-60; Brown, William 1929-30; Brownlee, John 1982-83; Brust, Chris 1979-82; Buckley, Bruce 1974-77; Bucknall, Steve 1986-89; Budko, Pete 1978-81; Bunting, Bill 1967-69; Burch, Michael 1987-88 (M); Burgess, Jason 1992; Burke, Edmund 1962 (M); Burns, Charlie 1962-63; Burrus, Amy 1994-95 (M).

C Calabria, Dante 1993-96; Callahan, Peppy 1962-63; Campbell, Greg 1966; Carmichael, Billy 1920-22; Carmichael, Cartwright 1922-24; Carrington, George 1911-13; Carson, Coy 1948-49; Carter, Jippy 1951, 1953; Carter, Vince 1996; Cate, Arlindo 1933 (M); Cathy, George 1928-29; Chadwick, Dave 1969-71; Chamberlain, Bill 1970-72; Chambers, Bill B. 1973-76; Chambers, Bill L. 1970-72; Chambers, Lenoir 1912-14; Chandler, Stuart 1931-33; Cherry, Scott 1990-93; Chilcutt, Pete 1988-91; Choate, Page 1930-31; Clancy, Gene 1953; Clark, Buddy 1955; Clark, Rusty 1967-69; Cleland, Thomas 1930-31; Cobb, Jack 1924-26; Cochrane, Bill 1965-66 (M); Cohen, John 1976-77 (M); Cole, Emilly 1996 (M); Cole, Mervin 1948; Coleman, Bob 1968-69 (M); Colescott, Dave 1977-80; Coley, Woody 1975-77; Conlon, Martin 1961; Cooke, Mike 1962-64; Corson, Craig 1970-72; Cox, John 1971; Creticos, Soc 1944; Crompton, Geff 1974, 1978; Crotty, John 1958-60; Cuneo, Frank 1940; Cunningham, Billy 1963-65; Cunningham, Bob 1956-58; Cuthbertson, Reynolds 1917-19.

D Dalton, Julie 1982-83 (M); Daly, David 1980-82 (M); Dameron, Emerson 1930-31; Daugherty, Brad 1983-86; Davis, Hubert 1989-92; Davis, Larry 1993-94; Davis, Robert 1914-16; Davis, Walter 1974-77; Dawson, Bobby 1992-94 (M); Daye, James 1985-86; Deasy, Howard 1949-52; Dedmon, Lee 1969-71; Delany, Jim 1968-70; Denny, Jeff 1987-90; Devin, Billy 1924-25; Dewell, John 1944; Dillon, John "Hook" 1945-48; Dilworth, Ben 1938-40; Dodderer, Bill 1924-26; Doherty, Matt 1981-84; Donald, Doug 1972-73 (M); Donnan, Dick 1944; Donohue, Hugh 1959-60, 1962; Doughton, Ged 1976-79; Dowd, William 1914, 1919; Duckett, Chuck 1980-82 (M); Duckett, Ricky 1977-79 (M); Duls, Ferdinand 1911.

E Earey, Mike 1970; Edwards, Ben 1913-14; Edwards, Jesse 1930-32; Eggleston, Don 1969-71; Einstein, Bill 1953 (M); Ellis, Chris 1989 (M); Ellis, Mike 1986-88 (M); Elston, Darrell 1972-74; Elstun,

Doug 1988; Emmerson, Fred 1967 (M); Engle, Fred 1961 (M); Ervin, Jim 1994-96 (M); Erwin, Roy 1912; Erwin, Jesse 1920; Exum, Cecil 1981-84.

F Ferraro, Hal 1949-51; Fitch, Jack 1944; Fleishman, Adam 1985-87 (M); Fleishman, Joel 1957 (M); Fletcher, Ralph 1966-68; Floyd, John 1911; Fogler, Eddie 1968-70; Ford, Phil 1975-78; Forehand, Randy 1968-69 (M); Fox, Rick 1988-91; Freedman, Ellis 1943; Frye, Jim 1966-68; Fuller, Walter 1915.

G Galantai, Bill 1963-64; Garvin, Dick 1945; Gauntlett, Tom 1965-67; Gersten, Bobby 1940-42; Geth, Ed 1993, 1995-96; Gilliam, Gid 1944 (M); Gipple, Dale 1969-71; Glace, Ivan "Jack" 1933-35; Glamack, George 1939-41; Glancy, Gene 1953; Goodwin, Frank 1955; Grandin, Elliott 1916; Green, John 1930; Green, Winton 1922-23; Greene, Hilliard 1955-56; Greene, John 1989-90; Gribble, Dickson 1966; Griffith, James 1919-20; Grimaldi, Vince 1951-53; Grubar, Dick 1967-69; Grubb, Foy 1937-38; Grubb, Scott 1994 (M).

H Hackney, Bunn 1925-27; Hackney, Rufus 1927-29; Hale, Steve 1983-86; Hamilton, Jim 1947; Hanby, Howard 1921; Hanners, Dave 1974-76; Hardee, Robert 1927 (M); Harper, Puny 1929-30; Harris, Kenny 1990-91; Harris, William 1935; Harrison, Ray 1973-74; Harrison, William 1935; Harry, Eric 1975-76; Hart, David 1982-84 (M); Hartley, Dick 1943, 1947; Harvel, William 1926; Hassell, Pud 1964-65; Hassell, Ray 1964-66; Hayworth, Jim 1946-47; Hayworth, Lewis 1942-44; Henderson, Willis 1955; Henry, David 1932-33; Hensley, Marty 1987, 1989-90; Hines, Wilmer 1931-33; Hite, Ray 1972-74; Hoffman, Brad 1973-75; Hoffman, Gene 1996 (M); Holding, Graham 1916 (M); Holland, Gehrmann 1957, 1959; Holt, Virginia 1995-96 (M); Homewood, Roy 1913-15; Hopkins, Jerry 1989-91 (M); Howard, Curtis 1942 (M); Howard, Jimmy 1939-41; Huband, Kim 1970-72; Hudock, Jim 1960-62; Hughes, Red 1946; Hunter, Curtis 1983, 1985-87; Hunter, Henry 1943 (M); Hutchinson, Joel 1930; Hyatt, Rodney 1987-88.

I Isley, Mark 1984-86 (M).

J Jamison, Antawn 1996; Jenkins, Francis 1928 (M); Jenkins, Joe 1988; Johnson, Chris 1995-96 (M); Johnson, John 1916; Johnson, Laura 1992-93 (M); Johnston, Donn 1971-73; Jones, Bobby 1972-74; Jones, Charles 1932; Jones, Harry 1961-62; Jones, Holly 1984 (M); Jordan, Jim 1945-46; Jordan, Michael 1982-84.

K Kappler, Hugo 1949-51; Karl, George 1971-73; Katz, Art 1962-64; Kaveny, Paul 1935-36; Kearns, Tommy 1956-58; Kenny, Eric 1979-81; Kepley, Dick 1958-59, 1961; Kocornik, Dick 1954; Kohler, Norm 1947-48; Koonce, Donald 1924; Krafcisin, Steve 1977; Krause, Dieter 1961-63; Kuester, John 1974-77; Kupchak, Mitch 1973-76; Kuralt, Justin 1988-91 (M).

L LaGarde, Tommy 1974-77; Lancaster, Rob 1995 (M); Landry, Pearce 1994-95; Larese, York 1959-61; Leath, MacLean 1929 (M); Lebo, Jeff 1986-89; Lee, Kenny 1978-80 (M); Lewis, Bob 1965-67; Lifson, Al 1952-55; Likins, Paul 1952-55; Lineberger, Henry 1924, 1926; Lipfert, Benjamin 1918-21; Lisenbee, Chuck 1992-95 (M); Lobin, Ben 1955; Loftus, Michael 1947 (M); Long, Albert 1954; Long, Henry 1911-14; Long, Meb 1913-16; Long,

Morris 1933-34; Lotz, Danny 1957-59; Lougee, Edgar 1943; Lubin, Ben 1955 (M); Lutz, Loren 1976; Lynch, George 1990-93; Lynch, Percy 1918-19; Lynn, Clyde 1995-96.

M Madden, Kevin 1986, 1988-90; Maddie, Bud 1951, 1953-54; Mahler, Carl 1922-23; Makkonen, Timo 1981-84; Markham, William 1932; Markin, Walter 1945; Marks, Don 1943; Marpet, Artie 1929-31; Martin, Warren 1982-83, 1985-86; Mason, Jeff 1976-78 (M); Mathes, Albert 1940; May, David 1988-89; McAdoo, Robert 1972; McCabe, Jerry 1954-56; McCachren, Dave 1932-34; McCachren, George 1943; McCachren, Jim 1934-36; McCachren, William 1937, 1939; McComb, Ken 1961; McCord, Dean 1984-85 (M); McDavid, James 1958 (M); McDonald, Monk 1921-24; McDonald, Sam 1923-26; McDuffie, Lewis 1917; McInnis, Jeff 1994-96; McIntyre, Maria 1989-91 (M); McKee, Ernest 1937 (M); McKee, William 1935 (M); McKinney, Bones 1946; McKnight, Roy 1911-12; McNairy, Charlie 1995-96; McSweeney, Bryan 1962-64; Meekins, Ralph 1981-83 (M); Meroney, David 1937; Miles, Greg 1973-74 (M); Miller, J.J. 1992-93 (M); Miller, Larry 1966-68; Minor, William 1935; Mirken, Mark 1965-67; Mock, Bernie 1944; Moe, Doug 1959-61; Moe, Donnie 1966-67; Montross, Eric 1991-94; Moore, James 1931; Moore, Jim 1966; Morris, Billy 1926-28; Morris, Cliff 1984-85; Morris, John 1919-21; Morrison, Ian 1965; Mullis, Pete 1936-38; Murnick, Elliot 1963-64 (M).

N Nagy, Fritz 1943; Nathan, Mark 1948; Neal, David 1995-96; Nearman, Sherman "Nemo" 1947-50; Neiman, Abe 1922; Neiman, David 1930; Nelson, Melvin 1934-36; Newcombe, Arthur 1926; Norfolk, Ira 1945; Norwood, Michael 1986-87; Nyimicz, Dan 1948-49.

O O'Donnell, John 1972-74; O'Koren, Mike 1977-80; Okulaja, Ademola 1996.

P Paine, George 1941-42; Parrish, Lannie 1984-86 (M); Parsons, Kendria 1987-88 (M); Patseavouras, John 1951 (M); Patterson, Richard 1950-51; Paxton, Bob 1945-48; Pepper, Mike 1978-81; Perkins, Sam 1981-84; Perry, Henry 1917-18; Perry, Sidney 1922; Pessar, Hank 1940-41; Peterson, Buzz 1982-85; Phelps, Derrick 1991-94; Phillips, Bob 1951-53; Poole, Jimmy 1923-25; Poole, Grey 1958-60; Popson, David 1984-87; Poteet, Yogi 1960-61, 1963; Potts, Ramsay 1936-37; Previs, Steve 1970-72; Price, James 1927-29; Purser, Carr 1927-28; Purser, John 1922-23, 1925.

Q Quigg, Joe 1956-57.

R Radovich, Tony 1953-57; Rancke, John 1974-75 (M); Ranson, Lucius 1913; Redding, Frank 1952; Redmon, Herman 1913; Reed, Lindsay 1979-81 (M); Reese, Brian 1991-94; Reid, Ben 1971 (M); Reid, J.R. 1987-89; Respess, Ray 1963-65; Reynolds, Steve 1988-90 (M); Rice, King 1988-91; Ritch, Marvin 1911; Roberson, Foy 1939-40; Robinson, Lynwood 1982; Rödl, Henrik 1990-93; Rogers, Sam 1991-93 (M); Roper, Gary 1985; Rose, Bob 1940-42; Rosemond, Ken 1956-57; Rosenbluth, Lennie 1955-57; Rourk, William 1920; Royall, Kenneth 1940 (M); Royster, Chauncey 1931 (M); Rozier, Clifford 1991; Russell, William 1948 (M); Ruth, Earl 1936-38; Ryan, Fred 1949.

S Salvadori, Kevin 1991-94; Salz, Harvey 1958-60; Satterfield, Henry 1928-29; Scholbe, Roger 1946-48; Schwartz, Elliot 1959 (M); Schwartz, Ernie 1951-53; Scott, Charlie 1968-70; Scruggs, Boyce 1916; Searcy, Roy 1956-58; Severin, Paul 1939-41;

Shaffer, Charlie 1962-64; Shaffer, Dean 1981-82; Shaffer, Lee 1958-60; Shaver, Tony 1974; Shepard, Carlyle 1917, 1920-21; Shytle, Ed 1941-42; Sides, Robert 1927; Smith, James 1974; Smith, Julian 1941-42; Smith, Junius 1911-13; Smith, Kenny 1984-87; Smith, Larry 1992; Smith, Mike 1966; Smith, Ranzino 1985-88; Smith, Winslow 1931; Smithwick, Jim 1965-66; Snead, Jane 1985 (M); Spencer, Thomas 1934 (M); Spiegel, William 1949 (M); Sprague, Peter 1954 (M); Stackhouse, Jerry 1994-95; Stahl, Ed 1973-75; Stanley, Ray 1958-60; Stephenson, Travis 1992-93; Stevenson, Buster 1944; Stoen, Chris 1996 (M); Stokes, James 1956 (M); Stroman, Joe 1980-81, 1983 (M); Strong, George 1913; Suggs, Reid 1941-42; Sullivan, Pat 1991-93, 1995; Sullivan, Ryan 1996; Sutton, Ed 1955; Swartzberg, Fred 1948.

T Tandy, George 1914, 1916; Taylor, Cooper 1952, 1954; Tennent, Charles 1914-15; Tennent, George 1916-18; Terrell, Simon 1950; Thompson, Ben 1967 (M); Thompson, Clive 1945; Thompson, Loy 1930 (M); Thorne, Charlie 1949-51; Thorne, Taylor 1946-48; Tillett, William 1911-13; Tsantes, John 1949-50; Turk, Irving 1950; Tuttle, Gerald 1967-69; Tuttle, Richard 1969-71; Tyndall, Webb 1996.

U Upperman, Leroy 1970 (M).

V Valentine, Keith 1976; Van Hecke, James 1938 (M); Vanstory, William 1927-28; Vayda, Jerry 1953-56; Veazey, Dan 1975-76 (M); Vinroot, Richard 1962; Virgil, John 1977-80.

W Waddell, Charles 1973-74; Wakeley, William 1911; Wallace, Jack 1951-53; Wallace, Rasheed 1994-95; Walsh, Donnie 1960-62; Washington, Donald 1973; Watson, Bill 1939; Weathers, Virgil 1932-34; Webb, Charles 1960 (M); Webb, Ricky 1968-69; Webster, Bernie 1935-36; Wells, Darius 1950-51; Wenstrom, Matt 1990-93; White, Jim 1943, 1946-47; White, William 1949-51; Whitehead, Gra 1968; Wiel, Randy 1976-79; Wiley, John 1930; Williams, Donald 1992-95; Williams, Scott 1987-90; Williams, Shammond 1995-96; Wills, Eddie 1993-94 (M); Wilson, Don 1942 ; Winstead, Skippy 1953-54; Wolf, Jeff 1977-80; Wolf, Joe 1984-87; Wood, Al 1978-81; Woodall, Junius 1921; Worley, Dick 1938-39; Worthy, James 1980-82; Wright, Henry 1937; Wright, Robert 1913; Wuycik, Dennis 1970-72.

Y Yokley, John 1964-66; Yonakor, Rich 1977-80; Young, Bob 1955-57; Youngblood, Joe 1966 (M).

Z Zaliagiris, Tom 1975-78; Zwikker, Serge 1994-96.

(M)=Manager;

TRIVIA ANSWERS

1. Clemson, Georgia Tech, Maryland, North Carolina, North Carolina State and Virginia.

2. The McCachkens — Dave (1933-34), Jim (1935-36), Bill (1938-39) and George (1942-43).

3. Wisconsin Field House at the University of Wisconsin, Madison, Wis.

4. Luther Hodges, who served as Governor of North Carolina in the 1950s, was a reserve guard on UNC's team in 1916-17. In 1958, 11 members of the team attended a reunion at the Governor's Mansion, where the Governor showed off his rusty passing skills. His errant pass shattered one of the mansion's ornate chandeliers.

5. George "Raby" Tennant and Charles "Buzz" Tennant in 1916-17.

6. Howell Peacock.

7. On Jan. 30, 1903, between the "Professional Students" (graduate students) and a "College Team" (undergraduates).

8. Monk McDonald lettered for four years in football, basketball and baseball in 1920-24. He coached the team in the 1924-25 season.

9. Norman Shepard.

10. Dr. Robert Lawson, a physician, physical education professor and the director of Bynum Gym, built an outdoor court adjacent to the gym in 1910 so the newly formed basketball team could practice without soiling his gym floor.

11. The University of North Carolina Indoor Athletic Court.

12. Sprints — Cartmell was an Olympic competitor in the 100 and 200 meters.

13. Duke.

14. Bob Rose.

15. Paul Severin, in 1939-40.

16. He played "Beau Brummel Bones" in a production of "Midsummer Night's Dream" in grade school and the name stuck.

17. Nemo Nearman.

18. Four, in three cities — the Atlanta Auditorium(1921-31), Raleigh Memorial Auditorium (1932-46), Duke Indoor Stadium in Durham (1947-50) and Reynolds Coliseum in Raleigh (1951-53).

19. His 1951 St. John's team reached the NCAA championship game, making him one of only a handful of coaches to put teams in national championships in two different sports.

20. Larry Brown, UCLA in 1980 and Kansas in 1988.

21. The point man for Frank McGuire's "Underground Railroad "in New York, credited with bringing Lennie Rosenbluth, Tommy Kearns and other New York-area stars to UNC.

22. Billy Hathaway from Long Beach, N.Y., measured an even 7-foot, according to newspaper reports. He averaged 2.8 points and 5.0 rebounds in 15 games in his sophomore season in 1956-57. Hathaway left UNC after his sophomore year and transferred to Pittsburgh.

23. Dick Harp.

24. Joe Quigg.

25. York Larese, for his incredibly quick release of his shots.

26. Aaron "The Bagman" Wagman was the New York "fixer" who lured Tar Heel Lou Brown into the point-shaving scandals in the late 1950s and early 1960s.

27. Billy Cunningham.

28. "Smiles."

29. In 1958 for Kansas State.

30. Lou Hudson.

31. Larry Brown.

32. York Larese and Doug Moe in 1959-61 and Bob Lewis and Larry Miller in 1966-67.

33. Larry Miller of the Carolina Cougars, 67 points.

34. McAdoo was the first junior college transfer to play for a Dean Smith-coached UNC team, and he was the first Tar Heel player to leave school with eligibility remaining to enter the NBA draft.

35. Dave Hanners, Brad Hoffman and Ed Stahl.

36. Steve Krafcisin played for UNC in the '77 Final Four and for Iowa in the 1980 Final Four.

37. Al Wood, 39 points vs. Virginia in 1981.

38. Dudley Bradley in 1979, averaging an ACC-record 3.3 steals per game.

39. Eric "Sleepy" Floyd of Gastonia.

40. Warren Martin, 9 vs. Stanford on Dec. 20, 1985.

41. Warren Martin, on a pass from Kenny Smith, Jan. 18, 1986, vs. Duke.

42. Eric Montross.

43. The cello.

44. Michael Jordan for the United States "Dream Team" and Henrik Rödl for Germany.

45. Kenny Rogers, on April 12, 1986.

46. Pat Sullivan, in 1993-94, when he decided to redshirt, and in 1994-95.

47. No. 10, Lennie Rosenbluth; No. 12, Phil Ford; No. 20, George Glamack; No. 23, Michael Jordan; No. 52, James Worthy. Jack Cobb's jersey, with no numeral, also is officially "retired."

48. Two — James Worthy by the Los Angeles Lakers in 1982 and Brad Daugherty by the Cleveland Cavaliers in 1986.

49. James Worthy in 1982 and Donald Williams in 1993.

50. Three, in 1982, 1984 and 1994. Smith's Tar Heels have been ranked second twice (1972, 1987) and fourth six times (1967, 1968, 1969, 1991, 1993 and 1995).

COLLEGE SPORTS HANDBOOKS
Stories, Stats & Stuff About America's Favorite Teams

U. of Arizona	Basketball	Arizona Wildcats Handbook
U. of Arkansas	Basketball	Razorbacks Handbook
Baylor	Football	Bears Handbook
Clemson	Football	Clemson Handbook
U. of Colorado	Football	Buffaloes Handbook
U. of Florida	Football	Gator Tales
Georgia Tech	Basketball	Yellow Jackets Handbook
Indiana U.	Basketball	Hoosier Handbook
Iowa State	Sports	Cyclones Handbook
U. of Kansas	Basketball	Crimson & Blue Handbook
Kansas State	Sports	Kansas St Wildcat Handbook
LSU	Football	Fighting Tigers Handbook
U. of Louisville	Basketball	Cardinals Handbook
U. of Miami	Football	Hurricane Handbook
U. of Michigan	Football	Wolverines Handbook
U. of Missouri	Basketball	Tiger Handbook
U. of Nebraska	Football	Husker Handbook
N.C. State	Basketball	Wolfpack Handbook
U. of Oklahoma	Football	Sooners Handbook
Penn State	Football	Nittany Lions Handbook
U. of S. Carolina	Football	Gamecocks Handbook
Stanford	Football	Stanford Handbook
Syracuse	Sports	Orange Handbook
U. of Tennessee	Football	Volunteers Handbook
U. of Texas	Football	Longhorns Handbook
Texas A&M	Football	Aggies Handbook
Texas Tech	Sports	Red Raiders Handbook
Virginia Tech	Football	Hokies Handbook
Wichita State	Sports	Shockers Handbook
U. of Wisconsin	Football	Badgers Handbook

Also:

Big 12 Handbook: Stories, Stats and Stuff About The Nation's Best Football Conference

The Top Fuel Handbook: Stories, Stats and Stuff About Drag Racing's Most Powerful Class

For ordering information call Midwest Sports Publications at:

1-800-492-4043